LEADING WISELY IN DIFFICULT TIMES

Three Cases of Faith and Business

Michael Naughton and David Specht

FOREWORD BY LARRY C. SPEARS

D1521993

Paulist Press
New York / Mahwah, NJ

Cover and book design by Sharyn Banks

ISBN: 978-0-8091-4738-0

Published by Paulist Press
997 Macarthur Boulevard
Mahwah, New Jersey 07430
www.paulistpress.com

Printed and bound in the
United States of America

Contents

Foreword

The three case studies that make up this book are engaging, hope-filled examples of "seeing things whole" while making a difference as a servant-leader.

The term *servant-leadership* was first coined in a 1970 essay by Robert K. Greenleaf (1904–90), entitled "The Servant as Leader." Greenleaf spent most of his organizational life in the field of management research, development, and education at AT&T. Following a forty-year career there, he founded the Center for Applied Ethics in 1964 and enjoyed a second career that lasted another twenty-five years. In 1985, the Center for Applied Ethics was renamed the Greenleaf Center for Servant Leadership.

The thesis central to most of his work was simple, but insightful and timely. He wrote:

> Caring for persons, the more able and the less able serving each other, is the rock upon which a good society is built. Whereas, until recently, caring was largely person-to-person, now most of it is mediated through institutions—often large, complex, powerful, impersonal; not always competent; sometimes corrupt. If a better society is to be built, one that is more just and more loving, one that provides opportunity for its people, then the most open course is to raise both the capacity to serve and the performance as servant of existing major institutions by new regenerative forces operating within them. [1]

Greenleaf was beginning to draw together two seeming opposites: serving and leading. It was a fruitful and effective pairing, and a concept that resonated around the globe. Since 1970, more than a half-million copies of Greenleaf's books and essays have been sold worldwide. Slowly but surely, his writings on servant-leadership have helped to form leaders, followers, educators, and many others who are concerned with these issues, particularly within institutions.

But what does servant-leadership entail? Who *is* a servant-leader? Greenleaf said that the servant-leader is one who is a servant first and a leader second:

> It begins with the natural feeling that one wants to...serve first. Then conscious choice brings one to aspire to lead. The difference manifests itself in the care taken by the servant—first to make sure that other people's highest priority needs are being served. The best test is: Do those served grow as persons; do they, while being served, become healthier, wiser, freer, more autonomous, more likely themselves to become servants? And, what is the effect on the least privileged in society? Will they benefit or at least not be further deprived? [2]

Greenleaf provides the launching point for our deliberations. The words *servant* and *leader* are usually thought of as being opposites, but when two opposites are brought together in a creative and meaningful way, a paradox emerges. And so it is with servant-leadership. Standard practices are rapidly shifting toward the ideas put forward by Greenleaf, as well as by many others like Stephen Covey, Peter Senge, Max DePree, Margaret Wheatley, and Ken Blanchard, to name a few, who suggest that this paradoxical notion of servant-leadership is a better way to better organizations. Greenleaf's writings on the subject helped to launch this movement, and his views continue to have a profound, far-reaching influence.

Foreword

I have spent many years carefully considering his original writings; from them I have extracted a set of ten traits of the servant-leader that are of critical importance. Central to the development of any servant-leader is his or her commitment to listening, empathy, healing, awareness, persuasion, conceptualization, foresight, stewardship, employee growth, and community-building.

These characteristics are also at the heart of the three companies profiled in this book. These cases show what these servant-leadership characteristics look like in the day-to-day stresses of organizational life.

Servant-leadership is both a burden and an opportunity. We must bear in mind, as Jitsuo Morikawa has noted, that

> more than in the past, the fate or welfare of human life is powerfully affected by the institutions of society; in fact, the future is being largely shaped by these economic, political and social institutions of our culture, so that the role of institutions, the moral and social accountability of institutions, becomes perhaps the number one agenda in our historical enterprise.[3]

But how is such a sweeping agenda achieved? One of the unique characteristics of this book is how the authors view these companies in light of such an agenda using an organizational model called Seeing Things Whole (which is also the name of the business community united by these goals). I am honored to note here that I served as president and CEO of the Robert K. Greenleaf Center for Servant-Leadership from 1990 to 2007. There I sought to be supportive of one of their most important initiatives: The Theology of Institutions Project—Seeing Things Whole.

In his essay "The Need for a Theology of Institutions," Greenleaf wrote:

> I do not believe that the urgently needed fundamental reconstruction of our vast and pervasive structure of institutions can take place, prudently and effectively,

without a strong supporting influence from the churches. And I doubt that churches as they now stand, with only a theology of persons to guide them, can wield the needed influence. I deem it imperative that a new and compelling theology of institutions come into being.[4]

Greenleaf's objective is challenging yet fruitful for people of all faiths and philosophies. Since 1993, the organization Seeing Things Whole and Greenleaf's writings have drawn together dozens of researchers, including a number of business owners, seeking to build upon the original servant-leader concept. *Leading Wisely in Difficult Times* is a potent contribution to this ongoing work.

Leading Wisely tells the stories of three companies whose servant-leaders desire to see things whole as they address complex, practical problems. While the authors seek to encourage people to be who they are, and to act as whole human beings in the workplace (a very positive impulse), they also raise the fundamental question: Is it possible for a Christian business leader to express one's sincerely held faith in the workplace without coercing others, and to honor the rights and beliefs of those who do not share their faith in Christ?

My own conviction is that it is not only possible but necessary; and, that the true test of a Christian servant-leader in this regard may well be how he or she chooses to respond to those workers who hold different beliefs and who have the right to have their beliefs respected, too—to be who *they* are. Only in such an environment will they "grow as persons...while being served." Only in such an environment where great care is taken by the servant-leader will they be "more likely themselves to become servants," servant-leaders who take great care. We could hope for no more meaningful outcome than that.

—*Larry C. Spears*
(www.spearscenter.org)

Preface

This book came about from two principal sources. In 2005, Robert Ouimet approached me to research companies where faith played a major role in the formation of the business and to examine whether the practices and policies of such companies were distinctive. Soon after, I recruited David Specht from Seeing Things Whole to explore what a project like this might look like. Seeing Things Whole is a nonprofit organization that works with organizational leaders, clergy, academics, and others, to bridge faith and organizational life.

In 2006, Helen Alford, OP, and I organized a conference entitled "The Good Company" in Rome. Over three hundred people attended the conference from thirty different countries, representing over a hundred universities. Many participants noted the need for more case studies on the general relationship of faith and work. Soon after, Sr. Helen organized an international group of scholars from the United States, Europe, and the Philippines to start to write cases.

This book is a response to these two events. It serves as a mini-casebook, examining Christian leaders who are attempting to live faithful lives in difficult economic situations. We make the argument that, though faith is taken seriously by many leaders in business, their example is often ignored. Instead, our current academic culture reads business as purely secular, legal, and highly instrumental. Our three cases studies tell a different story. We conclude with a reflection on practical wisdom, which summarizes three important lessons drawn from our particular case studies.

Each case study begins with a short description of a dilemma perplexing the leader. In order to understand the problem at hand, we provide background to the situation by explaining the kind of company the leader is working in, as well as the faith dimension of either the leader or the founders of the company. This background description allows the reader to be more informed in order to address the dilemma at hand by connecting the specific situation to the larger culture the leader inhabits. The case then returns to the initial dilemma and how the leader deals with it. The case ends with questions for discussion.

The follow-up to each of the cases reflects upon the questions of the prior chapter, bringing in theological sources for reflection. The point is not to simply provide answers to the dilemma, but to bring the reader into deeper reflection on the significance of human action in business, especially within a broader theological vision.

While a good question expresses a desire for an answer, a good answer to a good question should open up the person to deeper reflection rather than shut down further exploration. In a lecture she gave at St. John's College in Annapolis, Maryland, Eva Brann stated that a genuine question "does not dissolve when an answer is gained, any more than love necessarily disappears because its object is won." Her approach to good questions helps us to overcome the trite and rather popular story line that "there are no answers but only questions," or, "there are no right or wrong answers." If this were so, asking the question in the first place makes such an exercise futile.

There are answers, but they are usually not the sometimes shallow ones that we might initially express. The reflections we provide for each of the cases are an attempt to contribute to a unified moral outlook on business in light of faith. These reflections do not exhaust the moral exploration of the case, nor are they random reflections.

This attempt at moral unity is somewhat anathema to most approaches to cases, where each story not only stands on its own merits, but is seemingly isolated from every other and from the reader. One of the dangers of using cases is that they can fall into a relativism where the rightness or wrongness of the ethical decision at hand is found in the opinions of individual persons. There is no grand narrative of creation, sin, and redemption, but simply individual preferences described in discrete, unconnected stories. This approach to cases makes everyone poorer, because it severs us from each other and dissuades us from the reality that we are called to share a life together.

The principal concern of this book is to offer cases that overcome this temptation of relativism because they take in the whole of life. We hope these cases and reflections help leaders to become more human in the organizations they lead and in which they can help others to flourish. Our goal is to help leaders to see their holistic nature as body and soul, material and spiritual, faithful and reasonable, principled and technical. It is to help them to see things whole and to flourish in the daily, diligent practice of their faith.

We have been blessed to work with a variety of people in bringing forth this book. Liz Kelly, Leilani Briel, and Mary Kay O'Rourke have been invaluable in providing editorial help. Liz Kelly was particularly helpful in challenging our thoughts and arguments, which helped to tighten our thinking. Helen Alford, OP, has been a major driver of the overall case-study project, and without her organizational push this book would probably not have happened. We are also grateful to various people whose guidance and suggestions about these cases have been extremely generous: Anthony Brenninkmeyer, Dick Broholm, Jeanne Buckeye, Eric Donaldson, Jim Emrich, John Gallagher, Cathy Gamache, Ken Goodpaster, Bob Kennedy, Dean Maines, Tom Morgan, Ed Mosel, Stan Nyquist, Robert Ouimet, Kyle Smith, Bob Wahlstedt, and all those we have forgotten to list.

—*Michael Naughton*
    Director, The John A. Ryan Institute for Catholic Social Thought
    The Center for Catholic Studies
    University of St. Thomas, Minnesota

INTRODUCTION

INTRODUCTION

Telling the Whole Story

Today more than ever, the church is aware that her
social message will gain credibility more immediately
from the witness of actions than as a result of its
internal logic and consistency.
                    —JOHN PAUL II, *Centesimus Annus* (1991)

This book is an inside look at three companies and their
leaders who desire a deeper relationship between faith and work.
Their inspiration did not strike with bolts of lightning or vision-
ary dreams, but with whispers of grace, thoughtful conversations,
seemingly accidental encounters, and, most important, a long formation that was started in their families and nurtured through
their churches and education. While far from perfect, these leaders are *witnesses of action* who help us to see faith lived in business
today.

There are, of course, many stories of people of faith who have
failed to witness their beliefs in the world. Clergy and laypeople
alike have fallen short in living their vocations. Some have suc-
cumbed to scandalous sins of greed and lust, but most have accom-

modated themselves to the world, living as if God did not exist. They fall into pride or spiritual laziness (acedia), where God does not enter their stories even though they worship on Sunday. The miracle of the church is that it has survived these centuries despite such scandals and practical atheism. As ugly and as mundane as these sins are, they are nothing new in the history of the church or humanity, nor should they surprise any of us if we are honest about our own sinfulness and shortcomings.

What is new today is the ubiquity of such stories. Whether the story is about scandal or about herculean leaders, the larger "cover story" is that leaders don't need nor are they influenced by the gospel, the church, or God. We can easily buy into such a secular story line and lose sight of what God looks like in the world. But this cover story does not fully describe the various stories of faithful servants who pepper the landscape of business. These are not stories of perfection, of saints without blemish, but of leaders who are saints under construction.

These are stories not just about individual leaders, but also about how institutions are structured. There is an inextricable link between the character and quality of organizations and the fiber of those who lead them. Robert Greenleaf offered a similar observation in reflecting on the relationship between servant institutions and servant-leaders when he wrote, "If a better society is to be built, one that is more just and more loving, one that provides better opportunity for its people, then the most open course is to raise both the capacity to serve and the performance as servant of existing major institutions by new regenerative forces operating within them." And he goes on to acknowledge the essential role of faith and moral courage for those who would seek to lead as agents of transformation within their organizations: "I do not believe that the urgently needed fundamental reconstruction of our vast and pervasive structure of institutions can take place prudently without strong supporting influence from churches."[1]

The three stories within this book are of people who are trying to live faithfully in difficult times—times that are extremely competitive, complicated, globalized, and secular. These leaders are not motivated simply by wealth maximization, or enlightened self-interest, or some abstract social contract as often indicated by economic and management literature and textbooks. These self-centered and materialistic motivations create a very small world for people. These motivations do not generate the thoughtfulness, the care, the concern that the leaders within this book bring to their organizations. For these leaders, their faith creates a much larger world, a world in which God is at work, and where their own individual interests and desires are not the final word.

This is too often a story untold. Most business cases ignore the element of religious faith.[2] They fail to take it seriously as part of a leader's moral vision. What is ignored in the history of business is how many companies started with a vision that was informed by the religious faith of their founders, companies like Cadbury (Quaker), Malden Mills (Jewish), Herman Miller (Calvinist), ServiceMaster (Evangelical), Dayton Hudson, now Target (Presbyterian), Cummins Engine (Disciples of Christ), Mondragon (Catholic), and others.[3]

The leaders and founders of these companies and those in this book were nurtured in a culture in which a good life involved more than one person. The cultural institutions they were formed in, particularly the family, church, and education, instilled in them a theological vision out of which a moral orientation was developed. This moral vision caused these leaders to question their own individual self-interest and utility-maximizing inclinations, and seek to order their own good toward the common good in the institutions where they worked.

Such a cultural formation is not a guarantee of virtue or vice, but it will predispose future leaders to act in one way or another. If we have not been cultured in an environment where we have moral witnesses and servant-leaders, but instead in one where our individual preferences are primary, our consumptive wants prevail, and our careerist aspirations dominate, the chances of intending and attaining good ends will be difficult.

The point of these stories is not to say that the Christian religion is the only available means of humanizing organizations.

Christianity does not have a monopoly on good work and good companies. But Christian faith demands the baptized to be a light to the world. Christians, as well as all people, must speak from their center in such a way that allows others to do the same. They have to respect and protect the religious liberty of others. They cannot proselytize by imposing their beliefs on others, but they cannot at the same time abandon their own religious core in the name of tolerance, diversity, and pluralism.

While there are some organizational leaders who proselytize others at work and violate their religious liberty, we have found very few that do so. What we find more of in contemporary culture is a fear that prevents leaders from expressing any kind of faithfulness because they will be perceived as being too "religious," "dogmatic," or "fundamentalist." There are few labels in modern culture that are feared more than these. This label of being too religious paralyzes people of faith in organizations. They tend to accommodate whatever the values or strategies or recent consultant-suggested fad the organization has set in motion. Rather than making unique contributions to the organization, they settle into the lowest common denominator of organizational groupthink.

Tolerance, inclusiveness, and pluralism are very important values for today's organizations, but they are not strong enough by themselves to give people a robust vision of why they should work for the good of others. They are weak replacements to the theological realities of vocation and spirituality and to the moral principles of the common good and human dignity that have been taught, preached, and lived within the Christian social tradition. And when tolerance and diversity are seen as absolutes, they repress leaders and their coworkers from speaking from their core and offering organizations the richness of their religious faith, spiritual outlook, and moral center. This repression in the name of tolerance creates a very sterile and cold workplace. While bringing our whole selves to work presents dangers, not bringing our faith and moral life to work is far more dangerous in today's individualistic, consumer culture.

Whoever Tells the Stories Defines the Culture:[4] A Critique of Case Studies

While not every business case or story has to bring out the religious motivation of a person's faith, it is striking that so few do in a country where the majority believes in God. As educational institutions increasingly rely on case studies to introduce students into the profession of business and organizational life, cases are often written in such a way that ignores the larger cultural sphere from which leaders come, particularly the religious dimension of this culture. Case studies often lack the grand narratives that can help us understand why leaders act the way they do.

Case studies are not autobiographies, yet neither are moral decisions in business only a question of particular decisions and separate acts. They are not simply quandaries that leaders face once in a while, which is sometimes the impression one gets from case studies. David Lutz explains that case studies can give the impression that moral decisions within business are like the measuring chains that referees use at football games. Both the chains and ethics stay on the sidelines for most of the game and are only used when the situation is too close to call.

The moral life of leaders within business is not something that is tapped only occasionally. Rather, a deep moral ecology is at work. Leaders who are faithful will always be seeking a deeper integration of decisions and acts in their lives as a whole; otherwise, if they are not seeking this integration, they are often creating a divided life for themselves. This moral ecology reveals itself in the stories of their lives, their beliefs and intentions, and the institutions they live in. The moral decisions they make within business must be seen within this whole. Outside of this context toward *integrity*, this pattern to make our lives whole from its various parts, we cannot fully understand the moral quality of the decisions made. Again, the story of moral leaders is not just the discrete dilemmas they face, but a participation in a much larger narrative that connects them to others both now and in history, as well as to God.

7

So, when the story of business is told *only* in terms of secularity, *only* in terms of discrete acts, *only* in terms of individual choice, *only* in terms of the financial bottom line, it begins to create a culture of materialism, secularism, and moral isolationism, which cuts off the leader from moral and spiritual resources of faith to inform their decisions. Moral decision making then quickly becomes technical decision making, relying either on the law or the market as the principal resources to be ethical at work. As important as the law and the market are, they do not have the moral and spiritual resources to define what it means to be ethical in ways that humanize business. Without a cultural formation that occurs outside of business—that is, without the moral and spiritual formation that should happen in families, churches, and schools— business will tend to be monopolized either by legalism or by the instrumental values of the market (profitability, efficiency, and productivity).

In terms of the *law*, businesses driven by rules and codes run the danger of reducing ethical conduct to extrinsic demands imposed upon the organization and the leader. The moral life becomes a series of obligations, which can easily lead to legalism and minimalism and eventually to businesses becoming morally cold and sterile places. When one begins to obey rules, codes, or even commandments, it is never merely a static state. One may come to obedience of the law in duty, which is a good and important move, but if one does not begin to then move to love, such obedience leads to rigidity, minimalism, and legalism. The law by itself will always turn into a love grown cold. "Love does not inquire how far it *must* go, but how far it *may* go."[5] To simply observe a code of conduct and to reduce morality to following rules will eventually undermine the very code that is put in place, since compliance or duties to codes do not have the capacity, by themselves, to sustain one's obligation to them.

In terms of the *market*, businesses must be profitable, efficient, and productive, otherwise they die. But when these important qualities of a business are seen as ends rather than means, the business takes on a culture that gives way to the cold, pragmatic calculations of utility. Much of our current financial crisis can be explained by the over-confidence in financial engineering to maximize shareholder wealth. Business leaders were increasingly seeing themselves as technicians where faith and virtue were radically discounted in running the business. Business was seemingly not about moral judgment, but about economic calculations.

This moral discounting created a very small world for business leaders, which created the conditions for greed to dominate. As Dee Hock, former chief of VISA, explained, it is "not that people value money more but that they value everything else so much less—not that they are greedier, but that they have no other values to keep greed in check."[6] Thomas Aquinas explained over 750 years ago that evil and sin are always a matter of a deprivation of the good, a reduction of it. When business is seen only in terms of profit, efficiency, or legal compliance, we do not have the wrong values, but a disordering of goods that leads to vice. When we have discarded morality and spirituality from business, we have created the conditions for vice to dominate.

What faith illuminates for the leader is that the law and the market cannot fully explain his or her work. There is a larger configuration of life than business. The leaders we are reading about here are not just businesspeople; they are Americans, Christians, fathers, mothers, sons, and daughters. They are not just technicians or company people. Their responsibility in business life is not simply to some abstract shareholder, or customer, or organizational mission; more fundamentally, it is to the totality of their lives, of which God is central. To ignore faith, culture, and family is to distort business.

This is why our current financial crisis is embedded in a much larger cultural crisis, where we have lost our moral compass. As a result, leaders can no longer order the good of the corporation to the common good. This cultural crisis will not be solved through more complicated financial formulas and market techniques or through more onerous legal restrictions. Nor, quite frankly, will it be solved through better explanations of abstract philosophical tenets of utilitarianism, deontology, and the like, offered in most business ethics classes.

University professors who introduce business students to such ethical theories do so because they believe that students will become "critical thinkers" who can think for themselves. They teach students not what to think, but how to think. But this is part of the problem, not the solution. In universities, instead of connecting future leaders to the whole of their lives, we form them to be isolated from their culture, from their faith, from their families, and from their institutions. We are teaching them not to become persons in relationship to other persons, but to be individuals who not only think *for* themselves but who think only *of* themselves. This is not moral leadership but careerism and relativism of the worst sort.

Unless we address this larger cultural crisis, the humanization of business will always come up short. The stories in this book tell us that for many business leaders culture, particularly religious culture, plays a bigger role in decision making than the cover story we often read about. One of the principal underlying points of this book and its stories is that without culture, and especially without a religious culture that serves as the moral seedbed for ethical business professionals, we are failing to get at the roots of moral leadership within business. By themselves, the law, the market, and even moral philosophy cannot replace the work of culture. When religious, especially Christian, culture is at its best, it generates a moral life that orders the business realm in a way that then generates faithful companies that contribute to the common good.

What we propose here is a new kind of case study that takes seriously how one's moral courage, spiritual depth, and religious convictions shape the leader's ability to respond (response-ability) to the situations at hand. When we do this, we are taking seriously not just the particular stories of these leaders, but the grand narrative of the Christian story. It is the universal story of humanity that helps us to understand more deeply the particular stories of these leaders. This larger story also defines the culture, since it is telling us something about who the human person is, what they are created for, why they fail, and how they can move forward.

The individual stories of the leaders within this book are not theirs alone. The larger Christian narrative helps us to make sense of a deeper and more profoundly spiritual and moral drama of which we are a part, if we have eyes to see. When we see their stories in the context of the larger Christian narrative, we do not see discrete, isolated choices of individuals, but persons connected to other persons of the past, present, and future. We see a moral ecology at work where people who have been impacted by history and by institutions are themselves impacting history and institutions. The decisions these leaders make express not simply a psychological state of mind particular to them, but also a grander human story that plays out in a drama of the origins and destinies of millions of people worldwide.

REELL
PRECISION
MANUFACTURING

THE CASE

Should We Resort to Layoffs This Time?

Whatever you emphasize, you are in danger of overemphasizing.

BOB WAHLSTEDT, founder and board member of Reell

Reell's Difficult Choice

"In 2001 the high-tech bubble burst and we were particularly vulnerable because of our laptop hinge business," recalled Reell co-CEO Bob Carlson, shaking his head. "Our laptop hinge business had been growing rapidly. We had just made a significant investment in an expansion of our manufacturing capacity to keep up with the growth in the business, so the crunch hit us especially hard."

Signs of economic trouble for Reell began to first surface in the summer of 2000. "We couldn't figure out what was going on at first," Carlson explained. "Neither could our customers. One part of Toshiba was calling us to say that they needed more hinges, while at the same time, another part of Toshiba was calling us to cancel orders. We lost money in the fourth quarter of 2000 and then lost money again in the first quarter of 2001. In one year we lost 35 percent of the business—some seven million dollars in this strategic business line alone."

The company tried to improve sales, but the entire laptop market had dropped off. "Even if we had been able to develop new business," Carlson clarified, "it wouldn't have paid off for another year or two. Next we moved to cut everything we could—education and training, temporary employees, building improvements, contributions to the ESOP [Employee Stock Ownership Plan] and 401ks, and so on—in ways that wouldn't hurt our revenue-producing ability.

"We had a tradition of regularly gathering the employees for something we called 'pie day' to update them on what was going on with the business and the company. When times were lean, the employees knew right away because instead of enjoying pie at our meeting we would gather instead for 'cookie day.' So when we gathered that day around cookies, the employees knew that things were serious. Even after all of the cuts we had been able to identify, we were still left with expenses exceeding revenue and a large portion of expenses being payroll."

This was not the first time in its history that Reell had faced a significant shortfall in projected revenues. As a privately held and employee-owned company, Reell had a historical precedent of willingness to live with shrinking profitability even down to zero before putting the possibility of payroll reductions on the table.

By February of 2001, it was clear that the combination of the costs related to the recent investment in increased manufacturing capacity and the unanticipated revenue shortfall had brought the company to this zero-profitability benchmark, jump-starting a dialogue at the senior leadership level of Reell. The options on the table for reducing payroll were relatively clear:

1. laying off coworkers to achieve the necessary reduction in costs, or

2. implementing a program of reducing wages to prevent layoffs for as long as possible.

It wasn't at all clear which of these two options Reell ought to pursue. Further muddying the waters for leadership were several problems that had previously remained hidden beneath the waterline and now emerged as conspicuous.

"I recall our leadership conversations being rigorous with disagreement about what we should do," reflected Phil Billings, Reell's director of technology development. "My own perspective was that we should consider layoffs for several reasons. For one thing, the depth of the pay cuts necessary to make up the loss would affect the entire coworker community both financially and morale-wise. Also, there were some in the company who on a performance level contributed much more than others, making it seem unfair to distribute the costs of a pay reduction evenly. The truth is that this whole conversation brought to light problems at Reell that we hadn't sufficiently addressed. We hadn't been doing an adequate job managing the performance of our people, and we hadn't made an adequate commitment to a disciplined process of pursuing efficiency improvements."

"There was a concern," Bob Carlson agreed, "that if we elected to go with pay cuts instead of layoffs, we would run the risk of losing our best people, those best able to leave for other work elsewhere. While none of us liked the idea of layoffs, there was significant concern about the problems associated with implementing a program of pay reductions."

"The conversations were good, active, and intense, but we couldn't reach agreement," recalled Kit Mundahl, VP of corporate service. "Along with everything else, there was real uncertainty about whether the lost business would return and, if so, how long it would be. We really didn't know if the future would sustain our current workforce."

"Following extensive conversations," Carlson recalled, "Steve Wikstrom and I indicated that, as the co-CEOs, we would make the call on which path to follow."

Company Background

The story of Reell Precision Manufacturing in St. Paul, Minnesota, begins on October 13, 1970. Its three founders—Lee Johnson, Dale Merrick, and Bob Wahlstedt, all engineers—had been employed at the 3M corporation. Although they respected 3M, it had become increasingly difficult for them to see their futures there.

The first reason for this was their observation that their associates at 3M who were successful executives too often paid the price of family estrangement for career advancement. Lee, Dale, and Bob saw that, as one progressed up the company's ladder of success, relationships outside of work appeared to inevitably suffer. They witnessed fellow executives losing touch with their children, and they had no interest in repeating that problem in their own lives.

Second, they experienced intense profit-related pressures "to get the job done yesterday," often at the expense of the quality of their work. Racing to get product out the door frustrated their desire to feel proud about the quality of their work as engineers. They increasingly felt that they were not serving the needs of the customers and that they were becoming "company employees."

Having left 3M, they founded Reell as an engineering design manufacturing firm, specializing in the development of precision applications of their proprietary wrapped-spring clutch technology. By the mid-1990s, Reell had grown to a company employing more than 120 coworkers and had opened operations in Europe.

In the beginning, times were challenging and the three founders realized that, given the pressures facing their new venture, they were entirely susceptible to recreating in their own company the very same stresses they had reacted against at 3M. To avoid this, they asked a simple question: "What do we really want from our work in this new company?" They identified what they saw were four complementary aims:

- to earn a living

- to grow personally and professionally

- to be able to put family first
- to integrate faith and work

Moreover, they realized that if these four aims were important to them, they could reasonably assume that their employees might also have these same aspirations for themselves. This helped them to define "success" in their new company—a business and workplace where they could achieve all four aims with integrity. These aims were translated into a Direction Statement that articulated their moral and spiritual principles:

DIRECTION STATEMENT

Reell is a team united in the operation of a business based on the practical application of spiritual values to promote the growth of individuals and advance the common good for the benefit of coworkers and their families, customers, shareholders, suppliers, and community. Rooted in Judeo-Christian values, we welcome and draw on the richness of our spiritually diverse community. We are committed to providing an environment where there is harmony between work, our moral/ ethical values, and family responsibilities, and where everyone is treated justly.

The tradition of excellence at Reell was founded on a commitment to excellence rooted in the character of our Creator. Instead of driving each other toward excellence, we strive to free each other to grow and express the excellence that is within all of us. By adhering to the following four common spiritual principles, we are challenged to work and make decisions consistent with God's purpose for creation, according to our individual understanding.

DO WHAT IS RIGHT. We are committed to do what is right even when it does not seem to be profitable, expedient, or conventional.

DO OUR BEST. In our understanding of excellence we embrace a commitment to continuous improvement in everything we do. It is our commitment to encourage, teach, equip, and free each other to do and become all that we were intended to be.

TREAT OTHERS AS WE WOULD LIKE TO BE TREATED.

SEEK INSPIRATIONAL WISDOM. We will look outside ourselves, especially with respect to decisions having far-reaching and unpredictable consequences, but we will act only when the action is confirmed unanimously by others concerned.

We currently design and manufacture innovative products for a global market. Our goal is to continually improve our ability to meet customer needs. How we accomplish our mission is important to us. The following groups are fundamental to our success:

COWORKERS. People are the heart of Reell. We are committed to providing a secure opportunity to earn a livelihood and pursue personal growth.

CUSTOMERS. Customers are the lifeblood of Reell. Our products and services must be the best in meeting and exceeding customer expectations.

SHAREHOLDERS. We recognize that profitability is necessary to continue in business, reach our full potential, and fulfill our responsibilities to shareholders. We expect profits, but our commitments to coworkers and customers come before short-term profits.

SUPPLIERS. We will treat our suppliers as valuable partners in all our activities.

COMMUNITY. We will use a share of our energy and resources to meet the needs of our local and global community.

We find that in following these principles we can experience enjoyment, happiness, and peace of mind in our work and in our individual lives.

The principles of the Direction Statement represented a constant within the company's culture. They had a deep connection to the Christian faith of the founders as well as of many other Reell employees. For those who did not share this religious tradition, the principles still rang true because of their strong resonance with broadly recognized humanistic values and principles.

In addition to the Direction Statement, Reell also drew up another statement, one which was more deeply personal and more inclusive:

DECLARATION OF BELIEF

- We believe the dignity of every individual to be sacred.

- We believe life's highest purpose for each individual is to become all that she or he is created to be.

- We believe the highest purpose for the corporation is to make worthy contributions to the common good.

- Therefore, all activities, objectives, and policies are to be ordered toward individual development and the common good.

- Because economic success is essential for an environment that fosters human development and provides for the common good, we must maintain an orderly, efficient, and profitable organization and respect the dignity of every individual.

- Because many spiritual traditions speak powerfully regarding the conditions necessary to provide for the common good, foster individual development, and respect human dignity, we will encourage each other to draw wisdom from these traditions and from individual expressions of spirituality.

Company Practices

As the company evolved, managers and employees sought to embody these principles in particular practices and policies that they believed would create a community of work, thereby enabling coworkers to grow and develop. Like all organizational practices designed to reflect and deliver on cherished ideals, these were at times implemented imperfectly, and at times poorly. There was, however, a strong commitment in the company to "walk the talk." The relationship between principle and practice created a distinctive culture, one that helped its members to see more clearly the moral and spiritual realities in the practical problems facing the organization.

Some of the practices advanced by the company were the following:

• **Spiritual Support Group**. Early on, Dale Merrick recognized a spiritual dimension to their work and asked whether there were ways to more explicitly share this experience with other employees. They started a weekly Bible study that lasted for ten years. It was eventually discontinued because the meetings became less unifying and more divisive over conflicting interpretations of the Bible. Later on, several employees started a prayer group on Monday mornings at 7:00 a.m. Open to all in the company, it served as a time to "seek inspiration"; to share concerns with each other that dealt with personal, family, and professional life; and to strengthen a community of work by relating to each other in a more holistic fashion.

- **Silence.** When the three founders first started Reell, they would meet weekly and pray together over larger decisions. As the company became more diverse, the leadership of Reell revised this practice and began their meetings with seven minutes of silence as a discipline to "seek inspirational wisdom."

- **Outside Counsel**. When the company first began, the founders of Reell sought counsel from their church pastors to help them be faithful in the company they were building. As the company developed, it became connected with a group called Seeing Things Whole (STW). This group brought together Reell's leadership and leaders from other organizations to explore how their respective companies might best integrate the wisdom of faith, values, and organizational life. Leaders participated in these roundtables not as individuals, but as teams representing their company, so that the conversations that took place and STW's multiple-bottom-line way of understanding organizations could be brought back into the company and shape internal conversations within Reell.

- **Target Wage**. Reell hired new individuals at a competitive market wage. For production workers, however, the market wage often did not reflect a living wage. The company committed itself to raising their pay to a "target wage" within a relatively short period of time, by providing skills and training that increased their value to the company. The challenge for the company was to structure the work and to teach the individual the skills required to bring the work's "instrumental value" into line with the target or living wage.

- **Teach-Equip-Trust Style of Management**. Seeking to design better and more effective jobs through training and skill development, Reell redesigned their assembly line from a

Command-Direct-Control (CDC) style of management, where management and engineers made all the decisions concerning the conception of the assembly area, to a Teach-Equip-Trust (TET) approach, where employees were taught inspection procedures, equipped with quality instruments, and trusted to do things right on their own assembly line. As a result, employees decreased setup times for new products, reduced the need for quality inspection, increased overall quality, and reduced the need for supervision. By reducing these costs, the company not only was able to pay a living wage, but also created more humane work.

• **Monthly All-Employee Meetings (Pie or Cookie Day).** This practice began as a monthly celebration of employee birthdays and was later expanded to offer employees regular updates on what was happening with the business. It became an effective venue through which management delivered on Reell's commitment to "open-book management," sharing all financials with the employees. Building upon the Employee Stock Ownership Plan (ESOP), the meetings were used to foster a deeper sense of ownership within the company.

• **The Forum.** The Forum's primary role was to monitor the expression of Reell's Declaration of Belief and its Direction Statement in the day-to-day activities of the company. Members discussed improvements to existing policies/benefits or proposals for new ones. The Forum was comprised of the head of coworker services plus seven coworkers, whose selection was based on geographic location within the company. Prerequisites for Forum membership were three years employment at Reell and a demonstrated interest in the daily expression of the Declaration of Belief and the Direction Statement within the company.

• **Volunteer Time.** Reell encouraged its employees to give not only their treasure, but also their talent to the community. The company matched volunteer time with vacation pay.

• **Tithing.** Inspired by the biblical command to give the first fruits of one's earnings to the poor, Reell instituted a tithing program where its contributions to charity were at 10 percent of pre-tax earnings.

• **Equity Pay Ratio Indicator**. While there was no hard-and-fast ratio between the highest and lowest paid employees within the company, management was conscious of the fact that internal equity was an important reflection of its mission and principles.

• **Last Alternative Layoff Practice**. In economic downturns, layoffs were treated as a last alternative, resorted to only after seeking cost reductions in other areas.

Over time, the distinctive character of such policies and practices attracted and helped to retain employees at Reell. Historically, employee turnover rates ranged from 5 to 8 percent. At the same time, the spiritual and religious underpinnings of some of these practices were a source of uneasiness for, and created a sense of exclusion among, a few of Reell's employees.[1] There was also the problem of some of the practices falling into disrepair over time. For example, concerns were expressed that the training and development activities and budget did not keep up with the aspirations of the TET philosophy.

Company Business/Market Background

Reell sought to produce a product that its employees could be proud of and that would serve their customers' needs. The founders were all engineers who delighted in creating products in service to customers. The experience of working for 3M and a manufacturing rep business enabled them to understand the market and find potential improvements for existing products. All of them were keen on fostering excellent customer relations. They were committed to four particular goals:[2]

1. **Be Close to the Customer.** Reell was launched as a result of knowing the marketplace and how to serve the customer better than existing competitors.

2. **Design Excellence.** The first product was the result of good engineering; Reell offered a better, superior product. They were additionally fortunate in that

some of their products had long product lives, which did not require rapid redesigns.

3. **Quality and On-Time Delivery.** Reell manufactured a product with superior quality and delivered the product on time.

4. **Strong Long-term Relationships with Suppliers.** One aspect of that relationship was to pay suppliers within thirty days, even if that placed a hardship on the company.

The mission of Reell demanded a premium-price strategy to support a strong research and development (hereafter, R&D) budget. One of the more difficult pressures Reell continually faced was how to respond to customer pressure to reduce prices. In the late 1980s, Xerox, whose business provided 70 percent of Reell's revenues, demanded a major price cut on one of Reell's clutches, which would have hampered future R&D and employee benefits. The buyer was explicit: "If you don't reduce the price, there'll be no more business." Wahlstedt's only response was to say that their last shipment would be on time. Fortunately, the buyer was bluffing, and Reell was able to retain the business.

Wahlstedt viewed the buyer's request as unfair. He believed that it was right for Reell to make a fair profit. In return, Reell would not price gouge their customers and they would provide a high-quality product. A fair price included recovering costs and having reasonable profit that allowed for R&D to improve and develop new products. Reell left money on the table by not pricing to what the market would bear. They also walked away from money by not coming down on prices with what the market wouldn't bear.[3]

Ten years later in the late 1990s, these downward price pressures continued with even greater intensity.[4] Dan Stemm, VP of sales, felt that Reell could no longer resist price-reduction requests without losing major customers. As a small company, Reell had always been dependent upon a couple of very large firms such as

3M, Xerox, Kodak, Apple, Toshiba, Dell, and so on. At any one time, one customer could make up between 20 and 70 percent of the company's revenue.

At the end of 2000, Toshiba was one of Reell's largest customers with approximately 20 percent of Reell's revenue. Stem negotiated a price with Toshiba that reduced Reell's profit margins. Stem and others at Reell felt that failing to negotiate price reductions with Toshiba would lead to losing an important customer for its future. The laptop hinge business was growing rapidly, and there were clear signs that laptops in the computer market had significant growth potential.

Stem, along with some of the senior leadership, believed that such price pressures could actually be good for Reell. They would discipline the company to improve its purchasing practices and manufacturing processes and become more efficient in the management of inventory, supply chains, quality, rework, scrap, and so on. So while there might be a decrease in margins initially, in the long run, increased volume, followed by improved operational efficiencies, would make Reell a larger and more profitable company.

The price-reduction strategy with Toshiba increased Reell's volume significantly. In order to handle the increased volume, Reell expanded its manufacturing facility from 32,000 to 72,000 square feet and purchased expensive new automated equipment. The expansion and purchasing was financed by taking on $4.2 million of debt. Yet, even as the paint was drying on their capital investment, Reell saw a fast decline in Toshiba's orders, resulting in the need to reduce costs, including those related to labor. Reell's precarious situation, along with the economy slipping into recession, was reflected in its share price, which dropped from $100 to $80 a share between 2000 and 2001.

A Time to Decide

As Reell faced the difficult decision about how to reduce payroll costs, their own history was pulling them toward the option of utilizing pay cuts. Reell had utilized this option on four earlier occasions:

- In 1974, there was a period of about six months during which the founders took a 50 percent salary cut; the rest of the coworkers took an initial 10 percent cut that grew to 20 percent before it was over.

- In 1982, the shop workers reduced their hours (with corresponding pay reduction) for two or three months of the summer due to reduced production volume.

- In 1994, an across-the-board pay-and-hiring freeze was in effect from February through August.

- In 1996, a 10 percent payroll reduction was in effect from May 13 through September 13.

  1. No reduction in hours during the time of the reduction in pay.

  2. Voluntary time off without pay available only in the shop due to reduced production volume.

  3. Eighty percent of the ten percent cut was paid back December 6, 1996.

Although these four previous pay reductions were successful, this time the decision was complicated by uncertainty about whether *this* market downturn was different. There was a great deal of confidence at Reell in its technology and the capability of its people, but no clarity about when the market would regain strength, and the extent of the recovery. If the market did not rebound in the foreseeable future, Reell simply had too many people for the work that needed to be done.

Facing an uncertain future, management drew upon both principle and precedent in making its decision. The stories of utilizing pay cuts in the past as a way of avoiding layoffs contributed to the strong culture at Reell. There was a sense that choosing layoffs would negatively impact this culture—that it would break solidarity not only with one another but with Reell's legacy.

When the founders faced their first downturn in the 1970s, they drew upon both their experience and their spiritual principles in shaping their response. In particular, the Golden Rule ("Treat others as we would like to be treated ourselves") raised the question: "How would *we* want to be treated in such economic downturns?" The founders' response was to reduce their own wages in order to avoid layoffs. This did not come from a perspective of enlightened self-interest, but rather emerged as an expression of their commitment to allow the Golden Rule to become more than platitudes. In truth, they regarded this principle very much rooted in the gospel, which had a claim on their behavior as leaders within their company.

Yet, principles alone were not guarantees for economic survival. Reell faced significant issues. They were uncertain about whether business would return and to what extent, and about whether the workforce was too large for the resulting volume of work. They needed to actively diversify their customer base and develop new products on their technology application, as well as a better pricing strategy that would buffer market downturns. They needed to creatively improve operational efficiencies and more effectively address performance issues among employees. If not properly addressed, these issues could undermine a decision that would seek wage reductions and avoid layoffs. For example, the failure to address performance issues could potentially prolong wage reductions, which could wear thin coworker goodwill.

"During the time when Steve Wikstrom and I (Reell's co-CEOs) wrestled with the decision about whether to reduce the cost of Reell's payroll through layoffs or salary reductions," Bob Carlson recalled, "I kept thinking about another company named Tennant that I had worked for. It had been growing nicely, breaking into the Fortune 2000. Up until 1979, when faced with financial difficulties, Tennant had not resorted to layoffs, but had instead implemented pay cuts. In the 1980s, though, Tennant laid off employees and the company fundamentally changed. We lost the sense that we were all in this together. Our good humor and general sense of good spirits diminished. It wasn't that it became a bad company, but there was a real loss to the culture, and we wondered what it would take to get it back. It was like a really big wound that wouldn't fully heal." Other Reell employees had had similar experiences.

As an aid to their discernment about whether to resort to layoffs or pay reductions, Bob and Steve invited another member of Reell's leadership cabinet, Jim Grubs (VP of coworker services), to draft a statement examining the current dilemma in light of Reell's Declaration of Belief. Grubs was regarded by Reell's leadership as something of a theologian-in-residence. One of the explicit responsibilities assigned to his role was the care and nurturing of Reell's unique values-based culture.

On March 15, 2001, Jim responded to their request with the following:

FACTORS AROUND THE ISSUE OF WAGE REDUCTION VS. LAYOFFS

From casual conversations throughout this week I know that many, if not all of you, have been wrestling with this issue of reducing wages versus the laying off of some of our coworkers. I would like to briefly give you my perspective on this.

Initially let me say that while there is valid reason for either option, I am firmly of the conviction that we should continue with salary reductions. My point of reference is primarily our Direction Statement and Declaration of Belief.

As we all know, we have a history of wage reduction and I believe we've chosen this way because it expresses some of the basic Judeo-Christian values (most of which are present in other faith traditions). The value of *freedom to choose* is paramount to the dignity of the individual; it is an underlying principle of the Human Rights Charter of the United Nations drawn up in Helsinki, Finland. When you tell an individual he or she must leave, then you tear at the very fabric of their dignity—it is no longer a choice. They tend to view themselves as being judged of lesser significance/value. Practically speaking, we can no longer say, "We're all in it together." Volunteering to leave is a great deal different from being told to leave. In fact, it prevents the coworker from doing the very thing we've asked them to do and that is to "stay at the table"—stick with it/us and work this thing through.

Another primary value is that the *basis for community is the sharing of assets*. This particular value is a key ingredient for realizing our commitment to developing an environment of harmony between work and the rest of our lives. The policies and mechanisms within Reell Precision Manufacturing are literally riddled with evidences of this value. We work together in groups—constantly sharing time, energy, ideas, skills, tools, wisdom, monies, and so on. This idea of sharing assets was a hallmark of the Judeo-Christian community. We have shared well in times of plenty and, likewise, need to do so in these times.

The value of *"emptying" one's self for the sake of the other* is a premise for the highest form of love or, better said, compassion (to "suffer with"). It is the "sizzle" of caring for one another—very clear evidence that one person cares for another. In other words, when people see self-emptying behavior, they really get motivated to do likewise.

At the same time I am very mindful of the *Declaration of Belief*'s commitment toward the common good and our clear need to have a corporation that survives. For if we have no corporation, then we lose our ability to make "worthy contributions to the common good." In many respects, this is a good time for layoffs because the job market continues to be strong, we have strong resources to help with placement efforts, and we can better remain, compensation-wise, competitive with the market. Added to that, one might say, by laying off some coworkers, we get to choose who stays and who goes, thus better ensuring ourselves that we have the resources we need. We should never lose sight of this and continue to keep it as an item for consideration. However, I believe that we have continually demonstrated to one another an ability to creatively resolve situations, such as the one in which we now find ourselves, in a manner that is fair to everyone.

Overall, we must think this idea through very carefully because it represents a major paradigm shift in our corporate culture. It is a shift that moves us significantly, in my view, toward an environment of judgment rather than discernment, of fear rather than trust, of selfishness rather than community. It is a decision, which "above the waterline" may appear to make good economic and even leadership sense, but "below the waterline" creates a strong current of frustration, anger, and loss of hope. It is a decision that invokes a loss of freedom, loss of trust, and loss of compassion.

Finally, there are three important questions that everyone asks of each other: Can I trust you? Are you committed? Do you care about me? My answer? It is my belief we currently need to continue with the wage-reduction strategy.

> Thanks for listening.
> Jim Grubs
> VP for Coworker Services

"When Jim returned with his statement several days later," Carlson recalled, "Steve and I were really pleased. Jim's piece really captured well what many of us had struggled to articulate— our commitment to the people we worked with and our conviction that we must do everything possible before taking the measure of laying someone off. At that point, we were pretty sure which direction we were going. Before announcing the decision, we polled the cabinet twice—once about the decision itself, and again about their readiness to support the decision once it was announced. When it was clear we had their support to implement a program of pay cuts in order to avoid layoffs, we then wrestled with the question about how best to distribute the pain.

"Some advocated that we should all take the same percentage pay cut as a symbol of our all being in this together. In the end, we opted for a differentiated pay cut in which upper level management absorbed a twelve to sixteen percent salary reduction, with a lower percentage of seven percent for our salaried production workers, and management implementing their own pay cuts thirty days earlier. Those at or below the target wage were exempt from the pay cut."

These were the steps that Reell ultimately took:

- A 12 percent to 16 percent pay reduction for the Reell cabinet members became effective January 29, 2001.

- A 7 percent pay reduction became effective March 12, 2001, for most other coworkers and was phased in for newer hires, effective June 4, 2001. In all cases, those below the "target wage" (then $11.46/hr.) were not reduced.

- No reduction in hours during the time of the reduction in pay.

- Voluntary time off without pay became available.

- The third shift was eliminated on April 13, 2001.

- The Reell 401(k) match (up to 2.5 percent of salary) was suspended on April 23, 2001.

In October of 2001, pay was restored on a provisional basis. Pay cuts were lifted April 1, 2002, and the 401(k) match was restored then as well.

These steps have been added to and set down as a guide for any future economic down turns:

LAST-ALTERNATIVE LAYOFF

1. Provide lots of communication.

2. Get employees to take ownership in reducing costs, eliminating waste, enhancing margins, and generating revenue.

3. Institute a hiring freeze.

4. Reduce expenses such as education and training, temporary employees, building improvements, contributions to the ESOP and 401(k)s, and so on.

5. Institute pay cuts indexed to salary.

6. Institute layoffs when the above is not enough to stave off loss of profitability.

Discussion Questions

The options on the table for reducing costs immediately in light of the significant drop in revenue and increased expansion costs were relatively clear for Reell's leadership, but very complex. They could: *lay off coworkers to achieve the necessary reduction in costs*, OR, *implement a program of reducing wages to prevent layoffs for as long as possible*.

1. In light of Reell's decision to institute wage reductions, how would you assess the problem Phil Billings raised concerning poor performance reviews and the need for more-disciplined efficiency improvements? What are some possible unintended consequences of their wage-reduction decision in light of these problems?

2. How would you evaluate Reell's customer relations? Could they have done things differently with their customers that would have reduced their need to cut wages? With Reell's customers increasingly focused on price, how would you evaluate Reell's decision to expand, reduce prices, increase debt, and diminish margins?

3. What do you think was in danger of being overemphasized as well underemphasized at Reell, especially in light of the decision to go with salary/wage reductions instead of layoffs?

4. Finally, what would you have done if you were in charge? Lay out a decision strategy to address your shortfall between revenue and cost, and what you would do to possibly avoid this situation in the future.

A REFLECTION

Seeing Things Whole and the Golden Rule

Throughout this time of wrestling with the question of how best to reduce payroll, Reell's leadership drew increasingly upon the threefold understanding of their organization introduced through their participation in the Seeing Things Whole round-table. The threefold model articulates the connection between faith and organizational performance by describing organizations as dynamic systems comprised of three interdependent dimensions: *identity, mission,* and *stewardship.*[1]

Identity is focused internally on the experience of workers in the organization. It is how the organization arranges the character, culture, and quality of its life, including a host of issues such as job design, compensation, hiring, firing, evaluation, promotion, and training/development, and how these issues both model commitment to its principles and deal with the gaps between principle and policy.

Mission is externally focused on how the organization engages the world around it, especially, but not exclusively, its customers or clients. This is revealed by how it offers "a good," or a service, needed by others. Central to this dimension is a deep and active commitment to genuinely understand the needs of the world, and a commitment to move responsively to this understanding.

Stewardship focuses on how the organization secures and utilizes its resources (human, financial, and material) so that it becomes stronger, healthier, and better able to serve the common good. Essential elements to stewardship are sustainable profitability, continuous performance and productivity improvements, increased marketability for products, and so on.

Each of these dimensions and the concerns they represent are necessary to an organization's health and well-being. This is a multiple-bottom-line model of evaluating organizational success. Yet, while each of these three dimensions is essential to an organization's health, together these dimensions and the needs they represent are in an ongoing dynamic *tension* with one another.

When organizations address the tensions by overvaluing one or two of the dimensions at the expense of the others, they find themselves in a disordered state that makes it difficult for them to harness their full potential. Ken Goodpaster calls this disorder *teleopathy*—a disordering (pathy-*pathos*) of ends (teleo-*telos*), which is an occupational hazard of organizations and their leaders that causes them to forget their true purpose. The principal symptoms of *teleopathy* are fixation, detachment, and rationalization.[2] It was this insight about the nature of this normative and necessary tension among the three dimensions, and the disorders that result when these dimensions fall out of right relationship with each other, that was so helpful to Reell's leadership as they worked to better understand the situation they were in. We will highlight three possible aspects of this tension and disorder in light of the threefold model and Reell's situation.

Identity Fixation: Performance Problems and Efficiency Requirements

Reell's founders and leadership had taken great care over time to develop a robust organizational identity that, at its heart, sought to compensate for the familiar excess of a single-bottom-line model of organizational success (see the Direction Statement and the Declaration of Belief on pages 19 to 21). The single-bottom-line approach leans heavily on measurements of financial profitability as the primary indicators of a company's health. The leadership's commitment to see layoffs as a last alternative was one practice that contributed powerfully to Reell's identity. It added to employees' sense of safety, giving them confidence that their jobs were secure. This way of doing business had several benefits for Reell that were initially unforeseen:

- It increased creativity, leading to innovative product development such as the invention of the electronic clutch and the development of efficient production processes such as just-in-time and lean manufacturing.

- Having maintained its personnel, when demand did return, Reell was ready to ramp up at a much faster rate than their competitors who had laid off needed employees.

- Reell enjoyed strong retention of coworkers despite the fact that its salaries were lower than those offered by some larger competitors; historically, there was a sense that Reell was a company that rewarded loyalty with loyalty.

But, while Reell's commitment to its employees had created many benefits, it also cast a shadow.[3] As Bob Wahlstedt observed, "I've come to believe that the opposite of fear isn't only security. At least at Reell, the opposite of fear has sometimes been a creeping sense of entitlement on the part of some of our employees."

Because there had been no history of layoffs in response to previous economic downturns, some employees regarded the responsibility of responding to such challenges to be solely the province of management. As one manager observed, "Everyone knew that things were becoming difficult. However, only *some* people responded by putting in extra time, working to discover new efficiencies, or coming up with new ideas. Others continued to work as usual. It was as if they thought the difficulty we faced was somebody else's problem. This was especially evident once the wage reductions had been in place for a while. To be working like crazy to turn things around, while others around you who were paid the same amount weren't, began to feel unfair."

While wage reductions brought a strong sense of solidarity to Reell, their longevity was wearing thin the goodwill of certain coworkers, especially those who were putting in long hours. Pay cuts can strengthen a company culture, but, depending on how long they last, they also stretch and strain the culture, which can eventually become debilitating.

This awareness that some employees were working much harder and contributing much more than others led some to wonder whether the need for payroll reduction might offer an opportunity to "get rid of some of the dead wood." In talking about this possibility, there was general consensus among leadership that layoffs were not a good way to deal with previously unaddressed performance issues. It was a wake-up call to everyone, however, that Reell needed to strengthen the stewardship dimension of its life to more effectively manage performance and to build in accountability in order to simply remain viable. It was an opportunity to address what some people call the "Lake Wobegon effect," where everyone is considered above average. This effect is a result of the real and pervasive human tendency to overestimate one's work and talents and lose sight of one's lack of performance and the need for continual improvement in one's work.[4]

Mission Detachment and Customer Price Pressures

While Reell sought to create a strong and stable community of work in St. Paul, Minnesota, its product market was rapidly changing because of the global economy. Both its suppliers and customers were increasingly moving to China. This created higher shipping costs, more complicated inventory management, greater pressure for price reductions from customers, and so forth. Globalization created significant competition for Reell, while providing Toshiba and other customers more sources of supplies. This made it imperative for Reell to diversify its product mix and customer base in order to avoid the perils of overdependence on a few large customers. Whether Reell could have resisted the price-down pressures in the late 1990s as they did in the 1980s is a hypothetical question that cannot be answered. The benefit of hindsight, however, suggests that the failure to create enough customer diversification in a globalized economy compromised their ability to walk away from a customer's unreasonable demands.

Customers are the core mission of a company, but if they become king, if they possess too much power, they tend to disorder the company's identity and stewardship. Wahlstedt was able to resist the price pressures from Xerox in the 1980s. Stem felt that such resistance was not feasible in the late 1990s. Wahlstedt was critical of Stem's price strategy to expand the company based on lower profit margins. Reell's customers were increasingly viewing the laptop hinge market as a commodity, and consequentially their relationship with Reell became increasingly a price relationship. Wahlstedt and others always saw Reell's competitive strategy based on price, quality, and service. With one of the best quality hinges in the market as well as innovative engineering ability to solve customer problems, Wahlstedt did not want to compete on price alone and fall into a commodity business. Reell's strength was in specialty, not commodity, products. For Stem and others, the situation dictated a new strategy, which was the best chance for future success.

Not only was Reell under downward-price pressures, at the same time they were also expanding to capitalize on the opportunity represented by the growing laptop market. This created a significant dilemma. In expanding to keep up with the growth in their customer's business, Reell fell hostage to devoting an ever-increasing portion of their own resources to keeping this business and so began to be driven by their customers' demands, even when these expectations started to significantly erode Reell's own profitability and culture. Healthy profit margins were critical to their R&D plans, as well as to treating their employees well.

While the expansion and growth of any business is a good sign for the future, it is also an extremely vulnerable time in a company's life. Growth in revenues and market share do not always create more financial success for businesses. Top-line growth does not always result in bottom-line results. Actually, more businesses fail due to their inability to successfully manage the growth of their company than for almost any other reason. The strain on working capital—created by increasing inventories, growing accounts receivable, additional staff, more new equipment, the need for bigger space, the failure to create systems that can manage the increased production of the company effectively, and the failure to delegate—can all contribute to failure in a growing business.

On top of these internal pressures of the business, there are also the unpredictable swings of the economy. As a business grows, debt financing is easier to secure. But in the frenzy of growth, the company can take on a level of debt that cannot be sustained during the inevitable downturns that all businesses face. Many of the post–9/11 business failures were the result of funding their growth through high levels of debt financing. When the economy stalled after 9/11, debt-laden businesses could not meet their financial obligations.

All these factors highlight the unpredictability of the future. Whether Reell should have doubled its manufacturing space, increased its debt load, or reduced its prices is difficult to say without the benefit of hindsight. Very few people predicted the 2001 recession and no one forecasted the looming 9/11 disaster and its rippling effects on the economy. What is clear, however, is the critical importance of Reell knowing its customers and its market in order not to eliminate risk, but to better manage it. The entitlement problem at Reell discussed above could have contributed to a lack of attention to customers and the overall market. This inattentiveness probably contributed to Reell's misreading of Toshiba's customer orders. There was little product development occurring with their torque technology. Expansion on customer orders was done passively and not proactively: customers came to Reell, rather than Reell proactively seeking solutions for, and bringing them to, customers. Neither were executives traveling to customers. Again, this is not to say that uncertainty can be overcome, but if Reell's leadership had been closer to the customer, they may have had better foresight on the direction of their market.

While some of the decisions faced by Reell's leadership team in this case were shaped by assumptions about whether the business would come back, there is also the larger question of whether Reell was structured in such a way to meet the needs of this rapidly changing marketplace. Did they have the right people in the right jobs to serve the right customers? Were the processes, capabilities, and staffing levels structured in such a way to meet the current and future business needs of its customers? Were positions reexamined to better align specific coworkers with the needs of the company? All of these questions demanded great attention and a thorough understanding of Reell's customer and market.

Yet, with all this said, it is extremely difficult to have authentic relationships with customers when their only value is price. As the laptop hinge market began to change from a specialty to commodity market, customers like Toshiba and others began to detach themselves from Reell except in terms of price, which made it difficult, although certainly not impossible, for Reell to be connected to their customers.

Stewardship Neglect and Identity Rationalization

In hindsight, many of Reell's leaders, the founders among them, agreed that the company's emphasis on the quality of workplace experience for Reell's employees (*identity* dimension) came at the expense of an equal emphasis on practices concerning efficiency and profitability (*stewardship* dimension). While no one in the company would deny the importance of stewardship, there was a sense that when identity and stewardship came into conflict, identity trumped stewardship most of the time. The company was regarded as "faithful, ethical, and values based" when it behaved in ways that appeared to prioritize the well-being of coworkers over the concern for financial success. However, the company was considered to be "compromising or forsaking its values" when it placed high performance demands on its coworkers in response to financial pressures.

This bias against stewardship was not without basis. The founders of Reell left 3M because they experienced a fixation on stewardship at the expense of identity. Other employees who came to the company expressed a similar experience. Reell understood that the maximization of shareholder wealth was not its mantra. The company was conscious that it was different from most other companies. Their Direction Statement claims: "We are committed to do what is right even when it does not seem to be profitable, expedient, or conventional."

But, as Bob Wahlstedt put it, "Whatever you emphasize, you are in danger of overemphasizing." Reell's uniqueness created among some in the organization a subtle disregard for the independent importance of stewardship. It was implied that the stewardship dimension of the company would result from a strong identity. It was somewhat like Adam Smith's "invisible hand" argument, but reversed. Smith claimed that if individuals pursue their financial self-interest, the common good would result; some Reell employees suggested that if they were treated right, profits would result. This "results logic" disregarded a very important insight of the three foldmodel of Seeing Things Whole: that each of the organization's three dimensions must be independently and intentionally attended to and that, while they are interrelated, health in any of the dimensions does not automatically result from strength in another dimension.

This brings us to one of the most enduring challenges for organizations in relation to one of the most significant principles of the Christian social tradition—the common good. One dimension of the common good is to see it in terms of *foundational* goods and *excellent* goods. Foundational goods fall principally within the realm of stewardship—profits, efficiencies, productiveness, waste reduction, and so on. They are the goods that enable a company to survive. Excellent goods are connected to the nature of relationships and human development, particularly the growth of coworkers (identity) and the contributions a company makes to society (mission). In a welcoming statement that the founders of Reell used to give all employees, the relationship between foundational and excellent goods were metaphorically articulated:

> We do not define profits as the purpose of the company, but we do recognize that reasonable profitability is necessary to continue in business and to reach our full potential. We see profits in much the same way that you could view food in your personal life. You probably do not define food or eating as the purpose of your life, but recognize that it is essential to maintain your health and strength so you can realize your real purpose.

The founders of Reell recognized that if the pursuit of profits and other foundational goods was not taken seriously, an organization would weaken and soon collapse. Revenue, profit, and efficient use of resources, are necessary goals—and real goods—because they are the necessary means to organizational survival. In other words, foundational goods are always goods for something else. Nevertheless, if an organization is dedicated solely to profitability, then, even if it happens to pay good wages and to produce socially useful products, something about the organization is deficient. In particular, the deficiency is in excellent goods, which are principally found in the development of people through the relationships they have with each other. When employees, for example, join together to serve customer needs in an authentic way, their shared vision and values create a relationship with the customer.

This relationship between foundational goods and excellent goods brings us to an interesting dilemma for the leadership at Reell that can be captured in a rather simplistic moment of decision: pulling the trigger of layoffs too soon or too late. Laying off people too soon without seeking other alternatives to preserve people's jobs would weaken the bonds of communion within the company, since employees would experience little commitment from leadership (see Carlson's experience at Tennant). Laying off people too late would weaken the economic health of the company to compete in the future. Reell could err in terms of defect by not laying off and seriously harming the economic health of the company (stewardship). It could also err by laying off people too quickly and too extensively and seriously harming the culture of the company (identity). It is precisely why organizations need virtuous leaders who have the internal quality to make judgments that avoid the excessive and defective temptations in organizational life.

Conclusion: A Final Word on Purpose

Identity, mission, and stewardship are important dimensions of business, but there is one more word we need to engage if we are to understand what Reell's leadership was attempting to do. That word is *purpose*. Reell's desire to "see things whole" was motivated by the founders' religious conviction that the purpose of their work and of Reell was to do "the will of God." If identity, mission, and stewardship are the three legs of the stool, the purpose to do God's will is the seat that holds the three legs together.[5]

When we speak of the *purpose* of something, what we are attempting to define is our "deepest why": *to what end do we order our work?* For the founders of Reell, to speak of purpose or ends was to speak in spiritual terms, namely, to do God's will. Their work was inseparable from their religious convictions. They didn't do God's will at home and then follow their own economic interests at work. They left their former employer, we recall, because they wanted their work lives to be well integrated into their spiritual lives. They wanted to found a company that reflected deeper spiritual wholeness.

This religious language, however, made a few people nervous. The founders themselves were concerned about how this language might be misunderstood or mischaracterized. As these three founders sought God's will together, they did not think any one of them was God's spokesperson who had a direct link to God's will. Each had had enough experiences of failing to do God's will, as well as of encountering overzealous Christians who imposed their will as God's will, to know the inherent dangers of what they were proposing. But they were also aware that it was not simply about their will. They had a deep sense that their will as leaders was not theirs alone. They were beholden to a created order in which they were invited to participate.

John Kossett, one of Reell's engineers and an agnostic, said to Wahlstedt, "What do you mean by 'God's will'?" For Wahlstedt, the response to this question began with the Direction Statement: "Do what is right, do our best, treat others as we would like to be treated, and seek inspirational wisdom." Reell's response to layoffs was directly related to the belief in doing God's will. When the founders encountered economic downturns, they asked themselves, "What is God's will here?" The moral principle that arose for them naturally was the Golden Rule: "Treat others as we would like to be treated." This moral principle oriented them to see layoffs as a last alternative.

The Golden Rule came from their religious belief that each coworker had dignity because, like the founders, they were made in God's image, destined for the kingdom, and therefore to be treated with justice and compassion. Kossett did not accept the religious beliefs of the founders, but he did understand and acknowledge the Golden Rule and its practical expression of layoffs as a last alternative.

From a secular perspective, this brings up obvious questions: Why couldn't the founders simply state the Golden Rule and leave the religious language of God's will at church and home? Since we live in a diverse and pluralistic society, shouldn't Wahlstedt and the other founders of Reell have kept their religious beliefs strictly private? Shouldn't they have spoken only in terms of nonreligious language?

There is something profoundly ironic in this line of thinking. If, in the name of diversity and pluralism, companies like Reell must forfeit their forthrightly Christian character, then *diversity* and *pluralism* have become mere code words for secularized conformity. If pluralism is to be truly valued, then companies like Reell should be praised for both their religious language and their unique way of looking at layoffs. Reell made a good case that if one took the Gospels seriously, one could not look at layoffs as simply the economic activity of maximizing wealth. While people of a secular perspective may come to the same conclusion, it is not necessary that they do so. For Reell, doing God's will, living out the Gospels, entailed a necessary and special responsibility to keep its coworkers, even if that also entailed a certain degree of financial sacrifice.

It is important to note that the founders were clear that if they were able to bring their spiritual and religious beliefs to their business lives, then others should be able to do the same. In their Direction Statement, they said the following: "Rooted in Judeo-Christian values, we welcome and draw on the richness of our spiritually diverse community. We are committed to provide an environment where there is harmony between work and our moral/ethical values and family responsibilities and where everyone is treated justly." For Reell, religion and spirituality should be allowed to be expressed so long as it respects the religious liberty of others.

The other reason why the founders expressed the purpose of Reell in terms of God's will was the profound need for God's grace to run the company. It is not easy to run a business that would "promote the growth of individuals and advance the common good for the benefit of coworkers and their families, customers, shareholders, suppliers, and community." Within a marketplace that is increasingly competitive, driven by price alone, globalized, and secular, Reell would need all its coworkers to draw upon their own religious and spiritual resources if the company was to be what it hoped to be. Without these resources, these graces, Reell would most likely have become one more company imitating other companies in their pursuit of profit.

EPILOGUE

Ten Years Later

The Reell case study, like all cases, can give a sense that the company solved the problem facing it once and for all. Of course, this is never true. While one problem—laying off employees—was avoided, other problems were created, postponed, and continued, and new ones were already fast emerging on the horizon. Since the time of the case, the company has experienced a significant amount of further turmoil. Its move to expand into Asia brought revenue growth, but it also brought greater complexity, more volatility, increased price competition, and ultimately smaller profit margins. The last ten years also brought several changes in leadership. Reell's co-leadership model changed during this time, shifting to a single CEO. This change created tensions among longer tenure employees, the owners, and the new CEO. And in 2009, for the first time in its history, Reell implemented a series of layoffs. If it had not, the future would have looked quite dim.

Some of these difficulties were chronicled in an *Inc.* magazine article called "Paradise Lost," suggesting that this unique and special organization was losing its character and identity. The article hit on some truths, but failed to capture the full complexity of the dynamics at Reell. It assumed that the company *was* a "paradise" to begin with, which it was not. Yet, the article did bring out several important points: no matter how good relationships seem, they are fragile; no matter how stable companies appear, they change; no matter how virtuous people are, they are prone to stumbling and falling. Moreover, an organization is not an isolated and self-contained entity. It exists within the context of an ever-changing, globally competitive landscape. Therefore, change is constant, with both internal and external forces shaping the organization continuously.

Leading even the best of our institutions is very difficult and complex work. Periods of success and courageous initiatives are noteworthy precisely because they are not guaranteed to work forever.

If Reell were to go out of business next year, or make a radical shift in orientation, deciding that maximizing shareholder wealth was its sole purpose, it would not invalidate the important learnings that come to us from all they have ventured. Both good and bad companies go out of business. All sorts of institutions reshape their mission and identity. But even in the middle of these challenges and changes, there is freedom for leaders to be virtuous, principled, and competent to create good companies.

Reell has recently begun to write a new chapter of its story. In 2009, there was again a change in leadership, which brought significant redirection to the company. Kyle Smith, who moved from president to CEO, initiated a shift away from a strategy of growth through lower margin/high volume business and has been refocusing the company's strategy toward customers who find value in Reell's highly engineered and strong quality services, and not merely a price relationship. He has also worked with coworkers to reduce tensions and conflicts, especially those of longer tenure coworkers, and has developed stronger relations with all of the owners of the company.

In 2010, the company had one of its most profitable years in the twenty-first century, resulting in a 66 percent increase of stock value over 2009. All of this does not mean that the company is out of the proverbial woods. Future challenges involving strategy, profit, growth, and cultural aspects will always remain, and leaders will always have to endure the ups and downs of leading complex and volatile organizations. Their consolation is not just in the results, which may or may not materialize, but in the faithfulness and wisdom of their work, which is ultimately God's gift.

CASE STUDY TWO

ENGINEERED PRODUCTS

THE CASE

Doing Your Best When Your Best Efforts Fail

We spend a lot of energy wishing we were perfect. But we're not.

EARL STEVENS, former CEO of Engineered Products

Facing Imperfection in Organizational Life[1]

"Only seven years earlier we had agonized about how to respond to the pressure to move some of our manufacturing lines out of Massachusetts and into Mexico," recalled Engineered Products[2] CEO Earl Stevens, shaking his head. "Now we were back in the same room, once again wrestling with pressure to move the rest of the lines out of Massachusetts, this time to China.

"The price-down pressure from our customers—General Motors, Ford, and Chrysler—was extremely intense. They were in financial trouble themselves, rapidly losing market share to Toyota, Honda, and other competitors offering cars with superior fuel efficiency and quality. That last time around—when GM pressed us to relocate lines to Mexico—we had reasonable hopes of being able to protect our local manufacturing jobs through

55

replacing the departing lines with new product launches, and, as it turned out, we were able to do that. This time around, though, we didn't have any imminent new product launches, and it was becoming increasingly difficult to imagine how we could avoid laying off a significant number of our people.

"It was like waking up from the middle of a bad dream and discovering that you were in a living nightmare. We had always talked about our commitment to our employees. This was more than lip service. As a leadership team, we really cared, offered good compensation and benefits, including profit sharing, ongoing training, and education, and consistently recognized individual and team accomplishments. Some of our folks had been with us for more than twenty years. Many of them had families. The thought of telling them that we could no longer protect their jobs—that we would be laying them off—was unbearable.

"Our VP of human resources, Paul Owen, looked at me in the meeting when we came to the conclusion that we could no longer prevent these layoffs and said, 'Earl, I don't know if I can do this.' 'I know,' I replied. 'I know.'"

Earl had to face a dedicated and faithful workforce whose hard work and sacrifice were now going to be rewarded with a lay-off. How did it come to this? His own faith journey had directed him to create a business that would develop employees, serve customers, benefit communities, and reward shareholders, but now that holistic vision was coming apart. The story is a complicated one, but one that is becoming more common in American manufacturing.

Company Background

Engineered Products (EP) was founded by a Czech immigrant in Boston in 1909 as a tool-and-stamping company. The company was independent until 1969, when it was acquired by Standard Thompson. It was subsequently purchased by Allegheny International in 1979 and then by an Ohio-based firm in 1988. At that point, EP was a division with revenues of $30 million.

In the late 1980s, EP's leadership team made a strategic wager, based on their modest but steady growth and a series of recent successes in winning new business on the strength of product innovations: it decided to focus on becoming a larger and indispensable supplier for the automotive industry. Despite a concerted effort over several years, the firm had been unsuccessful in making inroads with any of the Japanese automakers or within other transportation industry segments, such as agricultural equipment. However, it had a growing and thriving relationship with General Motors, Chrysler, and Ford, the "Big Three" car manufacturers in the United States. Before long, contracts with these companies made up 85 percent of EP's business, and the future looked bright indeed.

CEO's Background

Earl Stevens' perspective on these emerging challenges was very much shaped by his own personal journey of faith. In the 1980s, Stevens had joined a Christian congregation whose Sunday worship bulletin featured the words *Ministers to the World...All the Congregation*. This phrase resonated with him. He heard sermons from the pulpit that spoke of the connection between faith and work. Prayers offered by the laity brought the workplace into the worship service. In comparison to his previous church experiences, this was very different.

Earl had grown up Catholic and attended its schools for twelve years. During this time, he had developed a strong faith and belief in God. In his newest congregational fellowship, he began to feel his faith in God reenergized, particularly around the concept that his leadership role in the workplace was ministry.

In the early 1990s, Earl began occasional conversations with Dick Broholm[3] in which the two explored the connections between Earl's faith as a Christian and his work as VP of sales and marketing at EP. "My faith journey had become important to me," Earl recalled, "but I noticed that there seemed to be a huge gap between my Sunday experience of being open, vulnerable, and warm, and Monday, where you had to be alert and guarded. Part of my journey here at EP has been around discovering a different model of leading and of organizational life, one that begins to close this gap by offering a different balance, one where we can be more human."

Earl began by inviting his leadership team to read and discuss books. In 1991, he had his team read Peter Senge's book *The Fifth Discipline*, with its ideas on dialogue, learning organizations, mental models, and systems thinking. Earl recalled the senior management off-site meeting at which the book served as the conversation's focus:

"I can remember some of them looking at each other, and one guy exclaimed, 'What the hell are we doing talking about this kind of stuff!' You have to understand, this was a room of engineers, and conversation about personal vision was for many of them an uncomfortable departure from our more familiar business talk. A few of them loved it immediately, but for the most part, they were somewhat cautious.

"What made it legit for most of them was that the next year we were joined at our off-site meeting by two folks from Ford's Lincoln Continental team who had joined MIT's learning lab. Parts of Ford were very much into the whole learning-organization concept, and at that point, we still had a very good relationship with Ford as a customer. When my folks saw how committed the Ford team was to these ideas, I think they said to themselves, "OK, maybe this stuff is alright after all." The next year, we expanded the leadership off-site meeting to include about thirty people, and we focused on Covey's *The 7 Habits of Highly Effective People*. By that time, folks were looking forward to our conversations, and we had given ourselves permission to engage one another in ways that began to close that gap I was talking about."

This journey of incorporating meaning and values into EP brought Earl to a group called Seeing Things Whole (STW), a network whose mission was to help bridge the divide between informed faith and organizational performance in order to serve the common good. "I was attracted to their model for a couple of reasons," recalled Stevens. "To begin with, it makes good organizational sense. It says we have to pay attention to multiple bottom lines—our relationships with our employees, the world around us including our customers and suppliers, and our resources—and assumes that the needs of these areas are frequently in tension with one another. This made sense of my day-to-day experience. The other thing I really liked is that, although STW's model doesn't use explicitly religious language, it has clear theological underpinnings, which helped me to feel a more tangible connection between my faith and my work at EP."[4]

This all happened during a period when EP was operating from a facility located within the inner city of Boston and experiencing profitable growth. In the 1990s, the company's expansion required them to establish a second division approximately twenty miles south of the city.

Expansion and Going Public

During this time, EP was a thriving company, and not only financially. While the firm's profitability fell within the upper quartile for its industry, EP's success was reflected on multiple bottom lines. In addition to being financially strong, EP enjoyed solid customer relationships, a robust supplier network, technically advanced product development, and a productive and committed workforce.

However, there were already warning signs. In May of 1992, Ignacio Lopez became the head of global purchasing at General Motors. At the time, GM was on the brink of bankruptcy. To help turn the company around, Lopez launched several dramatic initiatives, including tearing up contracts with GM's suppliers and demanding price-down concessions as a prerequisite for continued business. Although it wasn't apparent at that time, Lopez's actions initiated a trend that would profoundly reshape the industry.

Initially, EP was unaffected by these changes. The products they produced were usually small, often low-priced items. As pressure to reduce costs increased, the company introduced new products and product upgrades that helped to keep operating profits strong. However, during the 1990s, all three of EP's largest customers imposed a series of cost- and price-reduction measures that had a draconian impact on their supply chain. What began at GM in 1992 as a new form of cost competition evolved into a series of actions in which the Big Three found more and more novel ways to shed cost by placing it upon the shoulders of their suppliers. EP, however, did not succeed in widening its customer base and remained very dependent on the Big Three despite these negative developments.

In 1996, EP consolidated two divisions into a new modern and larger facility approximately twenty-five miles south of Boston. Earl Stevens was named general manager. The puzzle of consolidating the divisions and forming one leadership team was compounded by the additional challenge of moving from two separate hierarchical structures into a team-based environment. Management believed this change was vital to the organization's future success. Preparation and training for it had been underway for nearly eighteen months; still, the task was daunting.

Soon after the move, the CEO of EP's parent corporation convinced the company's board of directors to launch an initial public offering. Preparation of documents, historical research, development of the offering memorandum, and other related activities began in earnest later that year, creating another diversion for EP's leadership. The successful execution of the IPO in 1997 ushered in a transition from a private-company environment to that of a publicly held business.

Customer as King...and Dictator

As this growth was occurring, so was the influence of EP's customers. "In 1998," Earl recalled, "one of our customers added an additional requirement to a piece of business we had won. 'By the way,' they said, 'don't produce this product in the United States. If you're not in Mexico, we know you're not cost competitive.' So we began to produce in Juarez. This sent a shock wave through our company that we hadn't anticipated. On top of this problem, another emerged. Pretty quickly, our Juarez operation began to have quality issues. In an effort to straighten them out, we diverted significant engineering resources from other areas, turning attention away from the research and development that was critical to our future."

Apart from these problems, a series of demands from customers made EP's business increasingly challenging:

• **Externalizing the Cost of Tooling.** Historically, car manufacturers had paid for much of the cost of the capital purchased by suppliers to produce parts for their automobiles. Over time, they began to require suppliers to assume more and more of the cost of production tooling. This trend ultimately reached the point where suppliers were expected to both absorb capital costs and accept the risk of being "de-sourced" by a competitor, writing off the balance of the depreciation as a loss.

• **Externalizing Costs Related to Materials Management.** Automakers traditionally had maintained an inventory of the parts necessary to build their cars. Increasingly, suppliers were expected to maintain inventories to support just-in-time shipments. This expectation eventually transformed into a requirement that suppliers assume material management responsibility by monitoring stock levels at each assembly plant and ensuring these plants never ran out of the required parts.

• **Unilateral Actions.** Supplier relations within the U.S. automotive industry were steadily evolving into one-sided affairs. A particularly egregious example of this trend was Chrysler's decision to arbitrarily reduce prices to all suppliers by 5 percent and issue new purchase orders—take it or leave it. Similar actions were becoming commonplace, with contracts and other dimensions of the supplier-customer relationship focused exclusively on protecting the interests of the automakers.

• **Reverse Auctioning.** Over time, companies seeking to win a piece of business were required to compete with one another by lowering their bids against the clock, with the lowest bid winning the business. Stevens recalled one instance when EP's team nearly submitted a bid to sell Chrysler a part for less money than it would cost to produce. "I know it sounds crazy," he recalled, "but you have to understand that we were all caught up in the process. And there was more at stake than winning a particular contract. We were also seeking to increase our profile with one of our biggest customers. We saw our competitor's lower bid appear on the screen with only a few minutes remaining and were about to lower our bid again. Then we looked at each other and said, 'What are we doing? This is crazy!' Our competitor won the contract, but within a couple of years they went out of business."

• **Escalating Bidding Process Demands**. EP's primary customers demanded upfront cash payments or significant price reductions on existing products as the price of admission to the bidding process.

• **Price Reductions for the Life of the Product**. After EP received a particular piece of business through the competitive bidding process, the customer demanded that it guarantee an additional 22 percent of price reductions for the product over three years, or as much as 29 to 35 percent over five years. Carl Kenseth, EP's COO, recalled, "At one point we decided that agreeing to all of these price-down demands was simply bad business and that we would take a more nuanced approach. Rather than indiscriminately agreeing to them, we determined that we would examine each of these demands and agree to offer a reduction when we anticipated that we could reduce our costs without damaging our business. It wasn't long before we received a demand that we felt we couldn't say yes to, and indicated that we couldn't offer the reduction they were requesting. The customer immediately pulled the business from us and moved the product to a competitor."

EP's management team sought to address the continuing downward pressures on its pricing through a variety of measures. Besides trying to enter into the Japanese auto market, as well as into the large agricultural-equipment market, they sought a variety of efficiency measures. "We already had in place a cost-reduction program," recalled Earl, "and we were diligent about strengthening it through the implementation of the Lean and the Six Sigma production initiatives for reducing waste and increasing efficiencies in all parts of our operation. We worked to discover synergies with the sister division in our corporation, including the use of corporate purchasing initiatives to leverage our collective buying power. And we pressed our supply chain to also embrace the Lean and the Six Sigma initiatives that would increase *their* efficiencies and make possible cost reductions."

These customer demands and the company's response to them had a "cannibalizing" effect on the organization. Increasingly, EP found it more difficult to make itself a place where both employees could develop themselves and where shareholders could earn returns. Such demands also pressured EP to squeeze out cost savings from their own suppliers, which led to one trusted supplier going bankrupt.

During this difficult time of customer dominance, Earl Stevens translated the Seeing Things Whole threefold model (identity, purpose, and stewardship/fiduciary responsibilities)[5] into EP's strategic planning. Remarking on this move, Stevens noted: "It just made sense to me that if we were saying that we were a 'multiple-bottom-line organization,' then we needed to set goals that reflected not only our commitment to serve our customers, but also our concern for the well-being of our employees and for our fiduciary responsibility to shareholders.

"We grouped all of our major strategies from our long-term business plan under the headings of *Identity* (the gathered or shared life of the organization), *Purpose* (our work with customers and suppliers) and *Fiduciary Responsibilities* (our shareholders). This way of looking at the organization very clearly highlighted the tension among the stakeholders in these three areas and helped to guide our search for responses that took seriously the needs of all three dimensions of EP's life and constituencies. This, in turn, began to suggest a template—a kind of 'balanced score-card'—that we could use to gauge our performance."

ENGINEERED PRODUCTS' SHARED VALUES: THE THREEFOLD MODEL

Our Identity

The area of **identity** focuses our organization on these questions: Who are we? How does our organization structure the character and quality of our life together? Do we meet the full range of employee needs? This is shown through attention to

- the work environment
- how we recruit, hire, and dismiss employees
- how employees are motivated, disciplined, and rewarded
- how information is shared internally
- the rituals and customs that shape our organization's life

Identity Core Values at Engineered Products

Teamwork: We value a highly collaborative style of working together, in which our employees function as teams committed to understanding and responding to the needs of our customers through the development and production of products that effectively serve them. We continually seek integration among all teams within the organization.

Integrity: We value honesty and seek to create an environment in which people are committed to accurately assessing and describing both successes and failures, delivering and receiving both good news and bad.

Shared Costs and Benefits: We value all employees throughout the organization and demonstrate it by combining a competitive base wage with a value-added gain-sharing compensation plan. Everyone participates in the evolving well-being of the company by sharing in any value gained or lost resulting from the performance of the division.

Education: We value a commitment to education, training, and continuous self-improvement for all employees.

Recognition: We strive to recognize the achievements of all employees, for contributions both large and small, that help improve the quality of life within our organization.

Individuality: We understand that the primary source of our creativity and performance is the individual. We encourage each individual to make independent decisions in the best interests of the organization. We recognize and reward those who accept responsibility and accountability beyond the limits of their job descriptions. We encourage individuals to assume leadership in response to new challenges, threats, and opportunities, and will support each person in the face of associated risks and consequences.

❖❖❖❖

Our Purpose

The area of **purpose** focuses us on what we do, looking at the kind and quality of the products we provide to our customers. We justify our division's existence through attention to

- how well we define our mission

- how our organization projects itself publicly

- how we go about producing a product that is needed and valued

- how we serve our customer in the use of our products

- how the organization relates to our competitors and to the wider community

Purpose Core Values at Engineered Products:

Collaboration: Just as we value teamwork as a way of working together within EP, we seek it as well in working relationships with our suppliers and customers. We will adapt this philosophy so that it becomes operational in the context of the realities of our market.

Superior Quality: We serve the global marketplace through providing products of superior quality and value to our customers, delivered in a timely manner. We strive for constant improvement in our products and the processes through which we develop and produce them.

Acceptance of Change: We believe that ongoing change is a constant in life that must be embraced rather than resisted. We seek to anticipate the opportunities that flow from it and adapt in ways that enable us to serve excellently in their midst.

Core Competencies and Process Excellence: We seek to identify, nurture, and maximize the potential of our core competencies as an organization, as a way of focusing our service to the world around us. We understand that our capacity to serve well is dependent on the processes and systems that enable us to do our work and commit ourselves to strive for sustained excellence and innovation in our ongoing development of our processes and systems capabilities.

❖❖❖❖

Our Fiduciary Responsibility

The area of **fiduciary responsibility** focuses us on this question: "How do we do it?" It asks us how our organization utilizes its resources (human, financial, material) so as to sustain its viability over time while balancing the legitimate needs of all of its stakeholders. We do this through attention to

- how our organization secures essential resources for its mission

- how we allocate our resources consistent with our core values and the legitimate needs of all of our stakeholders

- how we balance stakeholder needs

- how our organization makes decisions and shares information

- how we mediate disagreements and balance contending issues

Fiduciary Responsibility Core Values at Engineered Products:

Sustainability: We seek to balance the quarter-to-quarter demands of the investment community with maximizing long-term profitability. This will enable us to fulfill our obligations to all of our stakeholders, including our shareholders, our employees, our customers, and the local community to which we belong.

Integrative Decision Making: We value honesty and seek to create an environment in which people are committed to accurately assessing and describing both successes and failures, delivering and receiving both good news and bad.

Shared Costs and Benefits: We seek to make decisions in ways that draw upon and attempt to integrate diverse perspectives within Engineered Products and to make the logic of our decision-making process explicit and transparent.

Growth: We orient ourselves toward growth through prudent risk taking. Our organizational environment will be one where all teams can creatively pursue growth strategies balanced with the commercial management of our existing business, within the context of corporate goals, divisional metrics, and team budgets.

2000—Running on Empty

When the "dot com" bubble burst in 2000, the resulting financial uncertainty led to a significant reduction in demand for cars and trucks. This placed even more pressure on EP and its parent corporation. Consequently, corporate leadership cut back spending on research and development, and suspended wage increases and 401(k) retirement plan contributions. These decisions hit EP particularly hard because its success was driven by its high level of activity in product development.

"So in 2002, when our customers pressed their demand that we begin to manufacture in China, it was déjà vu all over again," Earl reflected. "Only this time, because we had diverted our engineering resources from product development to solving quality problems in our production lines, we didn't have any new-product launches queued up to replace the product lines that would be relocated to China, and we didn't have alternative customers who could help us fill the gap."

Even while EP struggled to meet customer price-down demands, its parent corporation—now responding to stockholder expectations of quarterly improvements in earnings and share price—began to demand increased earnings from the division. In an environment of escalating costs, decreasing prices, and decreasing demand, EP was tasked with a return to historic levels of profitability.

Paul Owen recalled the situation: "It was relentless. No matter how hard our people worked, they never got to go home at the end of the day feeling like they had succeeded. Folks were feeling beaten up by our customers and, increasingly, by corporate. For every serious problem you solved, there were three or four more screaming for your attention. We knew that our employees were taking a beating, but couldn't seem to get ahead of the problem.

"At one point, I remember that we convened our top thirty leaders for a conversation about what we could do together, given the ongoing pressures, to improve the work environment for our people. There was a long pause, followed by a few comments about how it would be good to publish the company newsletter more frequently and how it would be nice if we could put aside more money for gift certificates to recognize employees, and then the dam burst. Someone began talking about the crazy pace, the latest horror story of being raked over the coals by Ford about a problem related to *their* having improperly installed our part, the worry about not having any 'can't miss' products in the pipeline, stories about other suppliers going out of business. On top of it all, they were very discouraged about the demand that we go to China. Like us, they had been battling to protect the jobs of our production folks, and didn't see how that would be possible now."

Over the past two decades, Stevens and others in EP's leadership team had developed a variety of practices and policies that had helped to cultivate and sustain a commitment to a human and values-centered approach to management in the increasingly fast-paced and challenging world. Some of these practices and policies were the following:

• **Training and Education**. Since the early 1990s, EP had a strong commitment to investing in its people through education. EP employees had access to technical training like Six Sigma that allowed them to become more successful in their on-the-job performance. They also had access to on-site courses like English as a Second Language (ESL).

• **Value-Added Gain-Sharing**. Since the early 1990s, in an effort to develop an approach to compensation that recognized the contributions of individuals throughout the organization by sharing with them the fortunes of the company, EP created an approach that combined a base wage with profit sharing that reflected the financial success of the company and the unique contributions of individuals to the success of their teams and business units.

• **Community Service**. Since the early 1990s, EP had a tradition of community service that included a partnership with an inner-city public school, and participation in service projects such as Habitat for Humanity and a walk to raise money for AIDS research. These activities brought employees together around a larger sense of purpose and meaning.

• **Brown Bag Luncheons**. Beginning in 1995, EP's leadership hosted lunchtime conversations with employees throughout the organization, sharing information—good news and bad—about how the business was doing, along with a word on new initiatives. These gatherings were also one of the occasions for publicly recognizing the contributions and accomplishments of employees.

• **Monthly Seeing Things Whole (STW) Leadership Luncheon Meetings**. Since 1996, members of EP's core leadership team gathered for lunch with STW's Ron Burgess on a monthly basis to discuss the challenges facing EP and how best to stay connected to what was ultimately important as they responded to these challenges. As Carl Kenseth, EP's VP of operations reflected, "For me, these conversations are about making sure that who I am here at work is consistent with who I want to be. I ask myself the question, 'If I were to go home this evening and tell my family about the decisions I made here today, would they feel proud of me?'"

• **Multiple-Bottom-Line Planning and Evaluation**. As mentioned earlier in this chapter, since 1997, EP leadership adopted an approach to planning and evaluation that focused their attention on three areas related to their company's well-being: the well-being of their workplace community, their relationships with customers and suppliers, and the financial health of the business. Their assumption was that all three were critical to the long-term health of the company and, therefore, deserved disciplined attention.

• **Integrative Decision Making**. First used in 1997, this practice was oriented toward decision making that reflected one of EP's core values. Integrative decision making is an approach to examining problems that seeks to insure that input and perspective from stakeholders who will be significantly affected by a decision are included in the deliberations that lead to the decision.

• **STW Roundtables**. In 2000, EP became a founding member of an STW roundtable in the greater Boston area made up of six organizations committed to integrating spiritual wisdom and values with their organizational practice and decision making. Each organization was represented by a stable delegation of leaders who gathered on a rotating basis in one another's businesses for half-day meetings. The host organization always presented an unresolved issue or challenge facing it, with participants from the other organizations serving as "temporary trustees" who seek to offer support, perspective, and wisdom. Every meeting included a "theological excursion"—a reading or teaching from a spiritual or philosophical tradition— that offered a different vantage point for seeing the organizational challenge being explored that day.

• **Fair Treatment in Layoffs**. The pressure to lay off employees over the last several years has become one of those occasions when the practice of "asking the question" has been important in clarifying what a values-informed approach to ending employment should look like. "It became clear to us," reflected Paul Owen, "that the way we approached layoffs and treated those who had to leave had a significant impact not only on those whose jobs are ending, but also on those who continue to work with us. The way we go about this can either strengthen or undermine our employees' trust in our leadership." At this point, EP's commitments to employees whose jobs will end included:

✔ Adequate notification—a minimum of six months if possible

✔ The provision of out-placement services

✔ Severance as an economic bridge into the future

✔ A merit/performance-based approach rather than seniority

• **Personal Best**. As EP's commitment to become a more human and well-balanced company grew, it became clear that deepening this effort would require a different kind of leadership training, one that invited participants to clarify their own personal values and grow in their effectiveness and capacity to maintain balance as they faced life's challenges. EP selected a program called Personal Best, which framed this commitment not only as a series of trainings for employees at all levels of the organization, but as lifelong journeys that required ongoing commitment and support.

Over time, the distinctive character of these policies and practices helped EP to retain employees in this highly pressurized environment; however, customer and shareholder pressure was making it difficult for employees to believe that they were still valued participants in this environment.

The China Decision: Facing a Dedicated Workforce with Bad News

As an aid to their discernment about how best to respond to the pressure to relocate part of their manufacturing lines to China and deal with the ensuing job losses in Boston, EP's leadership team sat "center circle" at one of the Seeing Things Whole round-table events described above to get support and perspective on this complex challenge.

At one point, those gathered at the meeting moved into three working groups. Each group focused on one of the three dimensions of the Seeing Things Whole model—identity, purpose, and stewardship/fiduciary responsibilities. The working group that considered EP's identity—the employees—was particularly dynamic, as participants joined EP leadership in worrying about the implications for those whose jobs would be lost as the result of the product line relocation to China. One decision facing EP's leadership was the question of when and how it should tell employees working on this line that their jobs would be moving to China.

This conversation took an unexpected turn when one of the participants, Robert Wahlstedt from Reell Precision Manufacturing, offered this reflection: "Your dilemma got me thinking about something Robert Greenleaf wrote in his initial essay, 'The Servant as Leader.' I want to preface it, though, by letting you know of the enormous respect I have for your management team and for the obvious integrity and great skill you are bringing to your leadership in a very difficult situation. I have some appreciation of the kind of very difficult market pressures you are dealing with here. We are also facing them in our own industry, but my sense is that they are not yet as acute as those you have been wrestling with in the auto industry. We are proud to be associated with you.

"At one point in his essay, Greenleaf observed that a central ethic of leadership is that of *foresight,* and said something to the effect that if you find as a leader that you are facing a dilemma with no good options to choose from, then it is almost certain that, at some point earlier on, you stood at a crossroads—maybe not recognizing it at the time—where your decision or lack of decision somehow contributed to getting you where you are now. Assuming that may be true, I wonder how it would be for you to reflect as a leadership team on when those moments of decision making might have occurred. With the benefit of hindsight, do you recognize now decisions that you were faced with then that, had you made them differently, might have—*might* have, not *would* have—unfolded in a way that left you with better options to choose from in this moment? The point in doing this is not to beat yourselves up, but rather to lay down any burdens that you might unconsciously be carrying around and to harvest any learnings you can, because I don't think these market dynamics are going to change anytime soon."

This particular comment by Wahlstedt stuck with Earl. As much as he felt pressured by his Big Three customers and now by outside shareholders, he had to wonder if *his* mistakes were also partly to blame for the impossible situation they were facing and the unavoidable move to China.

Several days later, Earl and the leadership team gathered their employees for one of their occasional brown-bag luncheon meetings. After offering a general update on overall market conditions, Earl told the employees that he knew many of them were anxious about the possibility of their jobs disappearing with the anticipated movement of product lines to China, and he wanted to give them as much information as possible to help them plan for the transitions that some of them would be facing. He shared with all of the employees the rough schedule for the staged movement of these lines over the course of the next ten months. He acknowledged that the next scheduled product launches were far enough away to prevent any smooth transition, and that consequently many of these jobs would be lost for the foreseeable future. He then outlined preparations the company was making to help those losing jobs to find new employment. As a result of conversations with other local industries, they had already identified a need for thirty employees with similar skill-sets.

Yet, Wahlstedt's comments the week before encouraged Earl to say more to his employees. Earl realized that he could not explain the move to China simply as a result of either the general and impersonal forces of globalization or the demands of customers, although both were a part of what had driven them into this corner. It was becoming increasingly clear to him that his decisions were also part of the reason that the company now faced this situation. He stood up and confessed to his employees:

"Obviously, this is painful, and we hoped it would never come to this point. We worked hard to prevent it, and while there are lots of good decisions we have made over the last several years, we have not been perfect. In looking back, there are a couple of decisions that, had we made them differently, could have helped us to avoid this.

"We were so enmeshed with the Detroit automakers that the new business path with them was always the easiest one for us to take. As a result, we neglected to continue to attempt to diversify with other global auto manufacturers. We also made only modest investment in the development of products for other transportation industry sectors, such as agricultural and construction vehicles. Again, while in looking back we found a lot to feel good about, those particular decisions I just described are ones we wish we had made differently."

This was a difficult moment for Earl as a leader. It was not easy for him to confess to his employees the strategic missed opportunities and its consequences for the workforce.

Reflecting back on these experiences, Earl commented on the value of the Seeing Things Whole event: "The group coming together to hold us in trust that weekend was incredibly important. Part of it was that it was a great group of folks, who brought so much wisdom and insight to bear on our situation. Although a lot of things we talked about we'd already been thinking about before the gathering, *this* time we were talking about our situation in the middle of a community. In hearing ourselves describe our situation to our 'temporary trustees,' we somehow felt the impact more powerfully and felt accountable to a wider community for doing everything we possibly could about it—beginning with telling the whole truth about what was happening and how we had arrived at that point."

Discussion Questions

1. How did Earl Stevens' faith influence how he viewed his company? How did he begin to connect his faith and values within the company? Do you find this type of integration healthy or problematic?

2. Describe how EP's relationship with its customers challenged Stevens' holistic vision of the threefold model (identity, purpose, and stewardship/fiduciary responsibilities). How did this challenge impact EP's commitment to its employees as well as to other stakeholders such as suppliers and shareholders?

3. What do you make of Stevens' confession to his employees at the end of the case? What mistakes were made by Stevens in his attempt to navigate this holistic vision?

A REFLECTION

Integrating Faith and Work

Earl Stevens' faith influenced how he viewed EP. While our general secular culture is weary and suspicious of religious faith, especially in relation to politics and business, Earl Stevens hungered for a greater integration of his own personal journey of faith with his work. As faith became more important to him, he was looking not for separation or compartmentalization of his faith and work, but a deeper unity between what he held most deeply in faith and what he did with most of his day.

Stevens' journey toward a fuller integration, however, was not just about him. He had no interest in imposing his faith and theological outlook on anyone; yet he also had no interest in living out his faith just on Sundays. One friend offered this advice: "Speak from your center and not from your boundaries, but do so in such a way that you invite and encourage others to do the same." Was this possible in a secular business? Stevens believed it was, but he needed to avoid two ditches. On the one side was a fundamentalism that failed to recognize the complex pluralistic situation of contemporary business and that had only one language with which to speak. On the other side was an aggressive secularism that cut faith out of the workplace completely.

Leading Toward Wholeness

EP had existed for nearly eighty years when Stevens first joined the business. The company had its own distinct culture and values. He realized that this would color the language and expression of the kind of integration he sought. An important part of Stevens' integration of faith and work would entail meeting people where they were.

EP was predominately an engineering company that tended to focus on technical language, so initially, Stevens began to introduce EP to authors (Stephen Covey, Peter Senge, and others) whose literature was becoming increasingly acceptable in business and whose work was also consistent with his desire to integrate faith, values, and business.

While Stevens accepted the company and its people where they currently were, as a leader, he also knew that he needed to take the company in a new direction if it was going to be able to see things whole. The work of Covey, Senge, and others served as an effective bridge to introduce the threefold model of Seeing Things Whole, and they did so in the following ways:

- Their writings were rooted in organizational experience, which made them relevant to his leadership group.

- Their writings, like the threefold model, freed people to raise larger questions than a financial or operational dominant culture could.

- While there was no explicit religious language that would cause any kind of awkwardness or sense of exclusion among EP employees, the ideas and language of these writings opened up connections that strengthened rather than marginalized faith.

Stevens believed the threefold model to be a tool that could be used by everyone, making sense to all his employees, while at the same time creating the possibility for them to think about questions of value, meaning, relationships, and purpose in relation to their work. It could allow them to tap into and integrate the deeper dimensions of faith and ultimate meaning into their working lives as they faced an increasingly tough competitive environment.

Threats to Seeing Things Whole and the Role of the Common Good

Throughout their years of wrestling with how best to respond to the mounting twin pressures to reduce costs and increase revenues, Stevens and EP's leadership were dedicated to another journey as well: the effort to embody an organizational commitment to multiple bottom lines that reflected concern not only for the company's service to its customers (purpose), but also the well-being of its workplace community (identity), and its profitability and strength into the future (stewardship/fiduciary responsibilities).

This vision to "see things whole" expresses what the Christian theological tradition has called the *common good*. Both the common good and Stevens' holistic vision resist the reductionist logic of single-bottom-line thinking that "it's all about maximizing shareholder wealth," or, "it's all about maximizing customer satisfaction," and so forth. Business practice is too complex to be reduced to simple financial formulas or marketing slogans.

In the Christian tradition, a business is a community of persons whose relationships and activities develop common goods over time. These common goods range from those that create the foundations of the business, like money, equipment, and business structures, to those that give meaning to the business as a whole, such as the community of work that is created there, the development of people within the business, and the service to the wider common good of society that the business provides. This tradition teaches that the goods we hold in common, especially those goods that build relationships and community, develop us into who we

79

are created to be. Through the input of numerous resources from various stakeholders, this entity, called a business, creates *goods* that people share in *common*. The threefold model describes these common goods in terms of identity (the goods shared among employees), purpose (the goods shared principally with customers, but also with suppliers and the larger community), and steward-ship/fiduciary responsibility (goods shared with shareholders, debt-holders, and so on).

To live out this vision of a business as a common good is not an easy matter, and it is full of tensions and difficulties. One of the principal challenges of businesses is to resist the increasing pres-sures to revert to a single-bottom-line orientation. For EP, the principal pressure, although not the only one, was coming from their customers. Businesses often claim that the "customer is king." Increasingly, EP's customers were acting like dictators. They held significant power over EP, *dictating* the terms of EP's prices, production location, supplier relations, and so forth, which began to negatively affect its identity through declining employee morale and stewardship through shrinking margins.

This invites us to reflect on a fundamental tension at the heart of the life of an organization such as EP: namely, that the very same systems that give a business like EP its life and purpose can also make it extremely hard for that business to operate in the way that it would like. Given that EP had not been able to widen its customer base, it became structurally embedded into the American auto industry. The dominance of the customer made it vulnerable to internalizing the best and the worst of that industry's cultural norms and logic.

In point of fact, EP's leadership team discovered that they had unintentionally contributed to the financial failure of a long-valued supplier by, logically enough, passing along to them the price-down demands of the Detroit Three. This supplier built the machinery for EP's production lines. It did an excellent job, and EP liked doing business with the firm. Moreover, with the migra-tion of manufacturing out of the United States, they were one of the few options for building these machines. EP's leadership called one day to check in with the supplier on the equipment for a new line that it was late in delivering. This was uncharacteristic of the company, so EP's leadership was surprised and wanted to get an update. When EP called, they learned that the supplier was just about to close its doors. It was deeply in debt and couldn't stay afloat. Without meaning to, EP had done to this firm exactly what Ford, GM, and Chrysler were doing to it. EP was asking the supplier to provide their machines for less and less money, to the point where they were still accepting EP's business but were now taking a loss. When EP learned this and realized how it had contributed to this situation, its leadership was distraught.

While EP was profoundly aware of the draconian demands of their customers, it took them a longer time to recognize that they were internalizing these same tactics in relationship to their suppliers. They were becoming more like their customers than they wanted to admit. The Christian tradition calls this the "subjective dimension of work," meaning that our work has an impact on us as human beings, on the kind of people and company we become through our work.[1]

The larger systems in which our organizations function influence us morally and spiritually, as well as economically. Just as, through our work together, we are called to build "structures of good" in our society, all of which come together as part of the wider common good, so we also find ourselves confronted by, sometimes without even being aware of it, deep-rooted, systemic evil, or what has been called "structures of sin."[2] These structures are perpetuated by individual choices that reinforce habitual patterns of behavior and strengthen policies that weaken the capacity of businesses to achieve the common good and to see things whole. When EP's customers reduced the focus of their whole relationship down to one variable—price—structures of sin set in that distorted the relationships. As the customers began to take over, they imposed almost unbearable risks and costs upon EP. Strained and broken relationships occurred not only between EP and its customers, but also between EP and its suppliers. A vicious circle can widen its malign influence across whole divisions of the economy.

On top of these struggles with customers, Stevens and his leadership teams were given another significant challenge when EP's parent corporation transitioned from being a privately held company to one that was now publicly owned. In each instance, EP found itself part of a much larger system whose own logic and urgent preoccupations very nearly overwhelmed EP's organizational life, and in the end threatened its very survival.

In one sense these experiences may be taken simply as yet another sobering reminder of the utter interdependence that binds us to one another on levels that are biological, social, political, spiritual, and economic. This interdependence is so fundamental that it is often relegated to the background of our awareness. And yet, our very existence is radically dependent on the extravagantly complex web of relationships that nurture and sustain us in all of these dimensions. Building the common good together is the moral dimension and heart of this interdependence.

Confessing Imperfection:
A Move toward Practical Wisdom

While Stevens and EP were overwhelmed by the scale and power of their customers' influence on their business, Stevens also came to the difficult conclusion that some of the strategic choices that he and the leadership team had made in the past were at least partly to blame for their current situation. Despite the pressures they faced, Stevens and his team continued to feel responsible for the well-being of their employees and their livelihoods at EP. While it was clear that they could not guarantee a set number of jobs for the future, it also became apparent to Stevens as he faced his employees that it was important to share a thoughtful and honest acknowledgment of the ways their leadership decisions had been imperfect. What Stevens recognized was that the power its customers had over EP's business and identity as an organization had been partly determined by the strategic decisions that EP itself had made.

Part of this imperfection came about from not mitigating the power of customers over EP. While Stevens and EP's leadership had tried to lay the groundwork for a diversification of their customer base, Chrysler, Ford, and GM continued to represent between 75 and 85 percent of their business. EP's leadership team recognized that the lack of customer diversification could ultimately prove a precarious strategy. They sought to overcome this by

- Expanding the automotive customer base by entering the Japanese market

- Developing products based on their existing technology for other transportation industry sectors, such as agricultural and construction vehicles

- Focusing on new, high-margin technologies, such as safety equipment

All three strategies were either under-resourced or had a very long introduction and approval cycle, and therefore fell far short of revenue and profit expectations. For example, when EP met with early resistance trying to sell to the Japanese, they did not persist, in part because, at the time, growth with the Big Three seemed endless. However, since they did not succeed in significantly diversifying their customer base, EP was held hostage to increasing customer demands, limiting the freedom of Stevens and EP to act in a manner consistent with the common good. In fact, EP ultimately became a participant in the methodical diminishment of the common good in the automotive-sector supply chain.

What Stevens confessed to his employees was essentially what being human is about, that we see things imperfectly and we act imperfectly, particularly concerning the means. We call this imperfection a lack of practical wisdom. This resulting lack of virtue was a consequence of incompletely implementing effective strategic means (customer diversification and new-product development with higher profit margins) that might have strengthened EP's well-being as a company and contributed toward the wider common good. While Stevens and his team certainly created a good company, their failure to develop it sufficiently well on all key dimensions of the business (and especially in the area of creating a wider customer base) left EP few strategic options to withstand the significant financial pressures being exerted by their customers.

In order to grasp the nature of Stevens' confession, it is important to understand what we mean by the virtue of practical wisdom, or prudence. Practical wisdom is the habit of recognizing good *ends* and choosing effective *means* to achieve those ends in changing and unique *circumstances*. It entails qualities of counsel, foresight, caution, and circumspection. Practical wisdom is concerned not only with what is right, but also that it is done rightly; not only with what is good, but that it is done well. It concerns what is important for all people: good decision making. It is an intellectual virtue, although it requires the three other cardinal virtues (justice, courage, and temperance) for its exercise. (See the Conclusion for further discussion on practical wisdom.)

Stevens found himself in a highly complex business environment. The challenges of the automotive industry, of customer mandates to expand globally, and of profitability pressures as part of a new public company all had significant impact on the strategies that the division chose to pursue. The virtue of practical wisdom is not an easy habit to acquire, both in terms of doing the right thing effectively in a global economic environment and doing it consistently over time. Stevens' lack of practical wisdom came, in part, from a long history of high margins and increasing revenue from well-established customer relationships. These so-called good times were in many respects dangerous times since they repressed within Stevens something he knew to be necessary—customer and product diversification.

Since it is not clear whether EP would have been successful with any of the alternative strategies, it would be unfair to judge previous choices in the light of current knowledge. For example, it is not clear whether Stevens and EP actually *would* have broken into the Japanese auto market if they had pursued it. They actually could have wasted a lot of time and money trying. It is a very difficult market to enter, since Japanese automakers, unlike the U.S. automakers, have very strong relationships with suppliers and do not dump them in order to gain on price alone. Stevens, nonetheless, wished that he would have pressed harder to have found out whether this strategy could have succeeded.

While growing in virtue involves admitting and learning from imperfect decisions, it is also just as much about handling the consequences of those decisions, especially if they have significant negative impact. Stevens felt it important for him to acknowledge, in a straightforward way, his leadership team's strategic shortcomings, since the consequences were quite disruptive and painful for his employees. Though he probably was not thinking about this at the time, "confessing" in this way was moving him toward greater practical wisdom.

Stevens, like all of us, was struggling toward ever deeper and more solid virtue, and, like each of us, he will continue in this struggle. Acknowledging and making our peace with this fundamental truth about organizational life and leadership (indeed, about life in general) will require organizational leaders to have the courage and humility to acknowledge when they haven't done things perfectly. In doing so, they offer to themselves and to those around them in the organization, the opportunity to begin to make adjustments, address the pressing challenges they face, and ultimately build stronger, more resilient businesses and become more prudent, virtuous people.

TOMASSO CORPORATION

Laying people off is by far the most fearful trial that a
business leader has to face. It's the most terrible pulver-
ization of the human and spiritual dimensions that
stockholders or managers can live through, assuming
that they have in the slightest degree hearts of flesh.
ROBERT OUIMET, chairman of Tomasso Corporation

A Practice-Based Approach to Integrating
Spirituality and Organizational Life

"When I was being interviewed for my job, I was asked to
read a small booklet that explained the philosophy of Tomasso,"
recalled Vince, Tomasso's finance director. "I was somewhat taken
aback by the explicit reference to both values and spirituality. I
understood that as part of the management team we would be
working on a special project that the owner saw as important to
Tomasso, but I was somewhat skeptical. I wondered what these
values of spirituality would mean, especially some of the specific
practices, like the expectation that we would follow up with any

former employees we had fired or laid off. I read about that and said to myself, 'I hope I don't have to live *that* one someday.'"

During his interview, Vince was impressed by Tomasso's emphasis on values, but at the same time was slightly dubious about its emphasis on spirituality. He was also somewhat wary about whether his new company actually did what it said. He could not have known then that he would soon be required to embody Tomasso's values.

When Vince started at Tomasso, the company was in the middle of struggling with significant revenue shortfall and, as Tomasso's new director of finance, he was confronted with the need to identify and implement cost-cutting measures:

"When I began, we were in the process of reorganizing to become more competitive, and within two months I had to lay off two people I hardly knew. I came in mid-May, and we let them go in June. They were two women in their fifties. Both had a skill set that didn't quite match up with what we needed. I had a couple of sleepless nights. Both had been with Tomasso for ten years.

"We did it immediately and without notice, because the financial pressure to take action quickly was real. The two women were surprised. My meetings with each of them were five to ten minutes long. The second person already knew by the time I came to see her. They both cried. It was maybe an hour from when I met the first woman until they both left the building. You want to be efficient, because there is no way we can make it right for them in that moment. In the afternoon we met with everyone to let them know what was happening and why. For me it was a horrible day."

Even though the company provided outplacement services, counseling, and a generous severance package for the two women, Vince found the experience one of the most unsettling and difficult of his management career. He wanted the dismissal of the two women to be as efficient and painless as possible, but something about the experience continued to make him uneasy. His vision of coming to a value-based and spiritually aware company such as Tomasso had not included letting go of two women who had been dedicated to it. What did this have to do with values and spirituality? What Vince did not realize at the time was that laying off the women was just the beginning of the story.

Company Background

Tomasso Corporation is a privately owned company in Quebec specializing in the production of familiar brand-name frozen dinners and hors d'oeuvres in Canada, the United States, and Mexico. The company was founded by Giovanina di Tomasso, who opened what quickly became a very popular restaurant, renowned in Montreal for its authentic Italian food. In 1956, she began selling frozen versions of this same cuisine, with the frozen foods eventually eclipsing the restaurant as the main business. Giovanina's two sons, Paolo and Marco, followed her into the business.

When, in the mid-1980s, the company won a large contract with Costco, the Tomasso brothers approached Montreal businessman Robert Ouimet seeking capital investment to finance the necessary expansion. His holding company acquired 100 percent of the Tomasso Corporation, with Ouimet himself becoming chairman and sole shareholder, while the Tomasso brothers continued to manage the business as president and vice president of operations. At this point the business had twenty employees.

Beginning in the 1990s, however, rapid growth necessitated a number of predictable changes that stretched and stressed Tomasso:

- The workforce had grown to more than one hundred employees.

- A conventional management structure with new managers replaced the familiar and personal hands-on management style of the Tomasso brothers.

- A modern frozen-food-product manufacturing facility was built at a new location.

- The larger workforce unionized, with tense management-union relations.

- A difficult adjustment to new production machinery negatively impacted customer service, with some customers reducing orders or canceling contracts.

- This, in turn, led to reductions in production and to wage cuts for employees, many of whom felt that their efforts went unrecognized and unappreciated by management. All of this put additional strain on management-employee relations.

- Tension increased between Ouimet and the Tomasso brothers over the kind of company they envisioned.

In 2001, when the Tomasso brothers decided to leave the company, long-term employees experienced their departure as a significant loss. With revenue and morale falling, Ouimet knew that the hire of the next CEO was crucial to the survival of the company and to the culture he wanted to create. After a careful search, Rob McKenzie became Tomasso's new president. He was given a twofold mandate by Ouimet: get the company back on financial track, and remake the culture of Tomasso into one that humanized and spiritualized its culture.

Owner's Background

Long before Robert Ouimet acquired the Tomasso Corporation, he had been experimenting within his own company, Ouimet Cordon Bleu (OCB), Inc.,[1] with various management practices that would harmonize spiritual and human values with the economic demands for productivity and profits. This effort grew out of Ouimet's desire to more profoundly connect his faith with his vocation as a business manager. Ouimet's deep personal faith as a Catholic and his disciplined economic approach to managing OCB, Inc., were like parallel tracks that ran side by side without ever actually intersecting. He experienced a problem all too familiar to businesspeople who are also persons of faith.

Some have described this as the experience of a divided life, a lack of connection between the sacred ideals and cherished values of one's faith and the pressing workplace demands of profitability, efficiency, and productivity. While, in his private life, Ouimet valued compassion, charity, solidarity, and authenticity, these values too often seemed remote from his business life, crowded out by the press for efficiency, competitiveness, diligence, and tough-mindedness.

Understanding the necessity of operational performance, Ouimet strongly believed that in order for these two worlds to be integrated, there must be specific management practices in place. Theory was all well and good, but irrelevant if not made operational. He wanted to find a management model that could put the principles of his Catholic faith into day-to-day practice. Catholic social teaching spoke of human dignity, common good, solidarity with the poor, participation, and subsidiarity, but what do these principles look like in a profitable and efficient business?[2] It was this desire for integration that caused Ouimet to experiment with simple practices that could carry out the meaning of such principles.

In 1997, Ouimet was able to take a sabbatical from OCB, providing time for him to better systematize his quest to integrate the spiritual and the economic dimensions of organizational life. During this sabbatical, Ouimet wrote a doctoral thesis more fully describing an approach to this integration. This lengthy thesis was summarized in a smaller volume that came to be known as the *Golden Book*, named for the color of its cover. Recognizing the need for a broader participation in the task of developing and implementing this approach, Ouimet began to refer to the effort as Our Project (Notre Projet).[3]

Prominent was a list of specific management practices that Ouimet recommended to members of Tomasso's management team, among which was the requirement that management follow up with former employees who had been laid off or dismissed.

Ouimet advanced fourteen management practices in all, as well as management tools for evaluating them:

PRACTICES TO CARRY HUMAN AND SPIRITUAL VALUES INTO THE WORKPLACE[4]

All the activities below take place on paid company time, and they are evaluated and assessed by three management tools, which are described after the practices.

1. **A Gesture**: On company time, a group of employees are provided an opportunity, once or twice a year on a voluntary basis, to make a humanitarian gesture to the larger community. This can take the form of serving at soup kitchens, prisons, nursing homes, and so on. After the activity, employees gather to reflect on the experience. Participating in "A Gesture" is done on company time and with no reference to the company's trademarked food products. Such a gesture transforms human relations in the organization by helping employees connect with each other by serving the poor and marginalized.

2. **Prize from the Heart**: Awarding a "Prize from the Heart" is aimed at promoting and rewarding particularly worthy behavior. Each year the prize is awarded to employees who everybody acknowledges as models of generosity, helpfulness, solidarity, and fraternity. To win the prize, people also have to have shown exemplary job performance. A committee of employees chooses the winner.

3. **Community Meals**: The company organizes two meals a year (before Christmas and summer vacation) that

bring together the entire workforce. The managers serve the food, which is a simple buffet. Over the years, this activity has helped to develop authenticity and humility in managers, as well as a spirit of solidarity, human dignity, and fraternity among all who attend.

4. **Support after Layoffs or Dismissals**: Managers who lay off or fire employees must contact those employees at least two times within a year after dismissal. The reasons for this practice are multiple, but principally, management needs to follow up to be sure the employees are all right and to see if they need further help. Another important reason for the practice is that the manager and employees have the opportunity to reconcile differences.

5. **Dinner of Four**: The hiring of all new people, and more especially managers, should be done—as a general rule—by including the person's spouse, or companion, at the very end of the interview process, but before any final decision. In this way, right from the beginning, the understanding of Our Project's spirit is reinforced, the spirit of collaboration and solidarity, which must exist in the company.

6. **An Annual Shared-Bonus Plan**: Once the company's annual financial budget has been met or surpassed, an annual bonus will be given to every employee—varying with each person's responsibilities and the company's performance.

7. **Testimonials**: Approximately twice a year, guest speakers, usually from outside the company, present reflections on their own chosen paths, existential situations, expectations, mistakes and successes, joys

and sufferings, or discoveries of certain human and spiritual values. These are strictly personal testimonials about their experiences that address moral and spiritual issues. The subjects dealt with have to have deeply human content.

8. **An Annual One-on-One Conversation**: These one-on-one conversations allow an employee and his or her immediate supervisor to share ideas frankly and directly about tension or breakdowns that may have occurred in their personal communication during the previous year. The discussions can develop values of confidence, solidarity, better understanding, and even reconciliation and forgiveness. This annual conversation, in a very special and essential way, complements the annual evaluation of professional performance. The one-on-one conversation should, however, never be held at the same time as the meeting dealing with performance.

9. **Meetings with a Manager**: Three people working in the company meet with a high-ranking manager for about ninety minutes to freely discuss subjects of the workers' choice. During the meeting no notes or minutes are taken. It is a time to freely put forward, in a frank fashion, issues that are on the minds and hearts of the employees. It is also a time for senior managers to hear what is occurring lower in the organization.

10. **Sponsoring**: Newly hired employees are mentored by an experienced employee in their departments who can introduce them to their colleagues and familiarize them with the organization's procedures, customs, and culture. Special attention is given to the unique practices described here.

11. **Interior Silence Before and After Certain Meetings**: In a climate of freedom, during official meetings of the board of directors, the executive committee, specialized committees, and other meetings, there can be brief periods of silence, sharing, reflection, and sometimes prayer.

12. **Spiritual Support Group**: This activity is primarily, though not exclusively, intended for members of the board of directors and the executive committee. On a voluntary basis, almost monthly, the participants are invited to a eucharistic celebration in solidarity with four religious communities that hold the company in prayer. The celebration is followed by a dinner with a shared reflection on a spiritual text.

13. **A Room for Inner Silence**: A room is set aside where employees can be alone in interior silence, relaxation, reflection, and, if desired, personal and silent meditation and prayer.

14. **Wall Posters and Annual Mottoes**: Free wall space in halls, meeting rooms, and offices is used to display posters that invite reflection on the fundamental values fostered by the activities of Our Project. All the wall posters promote different, but compatible, values. Also, each year a motto is voted on from a "bank of sayings" that those who work in the company themselves have suggested.

Management Tools That Guide and Assess the Human and Spiritual Practices: The above practices are constantly being adapted, revised, and at times deleted, since they are evaluated in light of the following tools:

1. **A Biennial "Climate" Survey**: Every two years an organizational climate survey is conducted by an independent, outside group to gather nonbiased information on the success, tensions, and failures of Our Project. More than twenty areas—such as communications, working conditions, personal development, salaries, job security, and so forth—are examined by the people working in the company.

2. **A Biennial Survey on the Efficacy of the Practices**: This second survey identifies which of the above practices are most appreciated and which ones need to be modified and/or replaced. The survey also helps to identify the primary values that employees see in the practice.

3. **Two Triennial Strategic Plans—Human and Economic:** Two separate but interdependent strategic plans are created every three years. The economic plan systematically guides the company toward the goal of being ever more competitive, efficient, dynamic, and profitable. The human plan systematically guides the company toward improvements and changes to the operation of each of the above practices so as to increase the personal development of those who work in the organization.

Ouimet believed that these and other practices would, if given time, contribute to the development of an organizational culture that was spiritually and humanly rich. The practices were designed to serve as a vehicle to carry human and spiritual values into the workplace, values that, in the past, seemed never to make it into the building. These practices and the values that accompanied them served as the means to humanize and spiritualize the organization.

Implementation Difficulties

For Ouimet, Our Project and its vision of reconciling long-term growth in human development with sustained profitability served as the integrating keystone for Tomasso. However, like most visions of any real consequence, this dream faced difficulties as it sought to become a lived experience within Tomasso.

The process of introducing the practices outlined in Our Project was slow and at times was met with cautiousness and even resistance. While there were multiple reasons for this caution and resistance, three stand out:

- **Leadership Resistance**: In many cases, existing management in OCB's companies—including the Tomasso brothers—never warmed up to the proposed practices and simply didn't implement them.

- **Fear of Proselytization**: In some instances, management and employees worried that there was a proselytizing intent underlying some of these activities. Initiatives that evoked this sense of caution included the establishment of a room for silence and reflection—initially introduced as a "room for prayer," an idea suggested to Ouimet by Mother Teresa when she visited the company in 1988. Quebec Province, where Tomasso is located, had experienced one of the most radical transformations from a very religious Catholic culture to a very secular one. Ouimet's religious and spiritual demeanor reminded many of the managers and employees of days long past, which led to a certain reserve and suspicion of his motives, particularly on the part of disaffected Catholics.

- **Inefficiencies**: Besides the worry about proselytizing, some managers saw the practices as simply an inefficient use of resources. For instance, when Ouimet decided to build the room for silence and reflection in one of the facilities, the managing director of the plant saw it as a waste of space and a possible haven for lazy employees.

These problems and others made Our Project and its associated practices extremely difficult to implement. It wasn't until the arrival of new leadership in the person of Rob MacKenzie that the practices began to shape Tomasso's culture. When Rob began his tenure as president, he affirmed these practices, along with the human and spiritual values they were intended to support. He made a commitment to institutionalize the practices, including the practice of following up with employees who have been laid off or dismissed.

Reconciling a Deep Wound

The impact of having to fire the two women was just beginning to fade for Vince when Rob MacKenzie approached him with the very last question he wanted to hear. "It was a month or so later," Vince recalled. "We were meeting as a management team and Rob asked, 'Have you called the two women yet?' I was stunned. I couldn't believe I had to call these people. I had seen their eyes, and one of them hated me. Rob said that he didn't need to know what we talked about, but that he did need to know that we had spoken."[5]

While Vince had no desire to call these two women, he nonetheless knew from day one that such a practice was part of his job description. "I kept putting it off. I thought on many days that *this* would be the day when I would call them, but then didn't get around to it and was grateful that I was busy. I kept thinking through what I would say. I finally did it in September—about three months after we had laid them off. I remember thinking, 'I'm going to do it…do my job.'"

The first call went relatively well. The woman had already begun another job. Although she was initially surprised, she was cordial on the phone and grateful for the call.

Vince knew that his call to the second woman would not be as pleasant. When he finally made the call, it was a mercifully brief but bitter conversation:

"I was very upset," she said. "I felt like an animal."

"Why?" Vince asked.

"I got thrown out, and I didn't even get to say good-bye to my friends," she responded.

"I'm so sorry that you didn't know that you could say good-bye," he replied.

"Well, I didn't think I could."

During the drive home that evening, Vince reflected on his day, wondering about all that had happened. While the first call had gone well, the second was every bit as painful as he had worried it would be. Once again he wondered aloud, "How on earth did I, a finance guy, end up with this as part of my job description?"

Vince's first follow-up call with his former employee wasn't his last. "I called again six weeks later, and the woman who'd been very bitter on the first call was more receptive," he recalled. "The first time I think she didn't trust my motives. She was still early on in the healing process. She volunteered more information about how she was doing. It was important for me to know that she was OK."

In retrospect, Vince talked about how the experience of making these difficult calls impacted him as a person and a manager. "Making these calls was really important to me. I found myself reflecting about this with Rob and my wife, and later spoke about what I learned from the experience in a management meeting. I learned how to act as a human being with others, giving people the respect they deserve. I had to do it, and hated doing it, but now I think that if I ever left to work somewhere else, I would do it there too. It made me a better human being."

Part of the practice includes not just calling the person, but meeting them face to face. "Later on," Vince recalled, "we invited these two ladies and several other former employees back to the company for breakfast. Both of them, including the one who was initially angrier, accepted right away. She had begun work in another job at this point, and was feeling better about things."

What surprised Vince was that some of the employees at Tomasso were very uneasy when they heard about the idea. They were afraid that the laid-off employees would make them feel guilty about still working here. In the end, however, all of Vince's staff decided to participate. "They were glad they did," Vince recalled. "They enjoyed visiting with their former coworkers and talked about wanting to do it again. This time the second woman had the opportunity to say good-bye to her friends."

Veronique, Tomasso's human resources director, elaborated further about the benefits of this practice. "It's good for our company. Managers who do this are impacted. It's not just that they dismiss people differently after doing this. I think they also hire people differently, manage differently, and evaluate performance more carefully and honestly."

Pierre, Tomasso's director of sales, recalled his own experience of following up with an employee he had dismissed. "It was one of my salespeople. He was doing an OK job selling—above average—but his focus on self and his own personal goals were damaging our sense of team. In the end, the dismissal was about his attitude and negative effect on the group. Because he was a good salesman, I knew he would go straight into another job once he left Tomasso, and that we would be seeing each other. So I knew I wanted to do this right.

"His reaction to his dismissal was OK, not surprised, because I had met with him about my concerns already on a couple of occasions. And I was right—he was going straight into another job, which he had already sought when we didn't offer him a promotion that he thought he was in line for. After he left, we met and I asked how he was doing and whether there was any way I could be supportive. We still see each other at sales events once or twice a year. I think if we hadn't already spoken with one another following his departure, these encounters could have been quite uncomfortable for both of us."

Discussion Questions

1. What do you make of Vince's struggle in initially calling the two women he fired? Was this an act of virtue or was it merely following orders? Are Vince and Tomasso any better off following this practice? If so, in what way? If not, in what way?

2. Should Vince have laid off the two women? And do you think the way he dismissed the women was consistent with the values of the company? Were there other alternatives besides dismissal?

3. How much do you think Ouimet can expect from his managers in carrying out the practices of the *Golden Book*? Do you think that Ouimet is imposing his faith on the management of Tomasso by making them follow up with laid-off and fired employees? What about the other practices mentioned on pages 94 to 98?

A REFLECTION

The Virtue of Practicing Reconciliation

Values in Tension

Vince, like most people, had little interest in seeing those whom he had laid off. Why open old wounds? But what happens when we leave conflicts unresolved? What happens to us internally and what happens to the world? What happens when we keep stuffing unresolved conflicts within us, when we keep saying time will heal these things, when we keep repressing conflict?

These questions raise a significant moral and theological idea that John Paul II calls "the subjective dimension of work." Instead of trying to dodge suffering, which is our first inclination, particularly in a consumer culture, we need to face it. But how do we face the difficulties of today's business organization? Are financial formulas, strategic plans, measurements, and so on, sufficient to support our being fully human and faithful in the middle of complex and morally challenging circumstances? Or do we need a moral and spiritual vision informed by specific practices to anchor and sustain us?

In the last ten years, we have seen a revolution of sorts in which businesspeople have been taking the relevance of their faith to their paid work more seriously. While most people of faith do not want to live compartmentalized lives, they find it difficult to imagine what an integrated life of faith and work looks like in reality. The practices developed by Robert Ouimet and implemented by the leaders within Tomasso provide an especially helpful model for bringing spirituality, values, and organizational life together in tangible and specific ways.

In truth, this dimension of concrete management practices is present to some extent in most organizations that are seeking to integrate faith, work, and business performance. However, among those institutions that have made significant progress in expressing a genuine integration of spiritual and human values within their daily operational reality, most have not incorporated the discipline of specific management practices in the way that Tomasso did during the past several years. Rather than specific practices, other organizations begin deductively with crafted statements of belief or the identification of explicit core values. The intent of these statements is to provide a spiritual or moral compass with which to guide the organization's policy and performance. The practices of the organization then typically emerge as management wrestles to discover ways of leading that genuinely reflect a commitment to the organization's espoused beliefs or values. Without practical expressions of spiritual and human values in the day-to-day life of the organization, the espousal of moral and spiritual principles risks giving rise to cynicism about the possibility of ever really overcoming the compartmentalization of personal faith and business performance.

Tomasso, of course, along with its concrete practices, also had the *Golden Book*, which identified a set of explicitly spiritual and human values for itself. It provided a conceptual framework that represented the organization's commitment to hold together the procedures of successful business performance and a workplace experience that aspired to a deepening of spiritual and humanitarian values. These did indeed exist at Tomasso, but again, the unique and leading edge of Tomasso's approach to actualizing this integration was decidedly practical and experiential, supported first and foremost by a carefully identified collection of specific management practices.

The experiential emphasis of Tomasso's practice-based approach had clear strengths, as can be seen with Vince's story. Nevertheless, this approach is not without its potential problems and tensions. In this last section, we will highlight three tensions that Tomasso and any other company that follows this practice-based approach will likely encounter.

The Difference between Virtue and Duty

In the movie *The Karate Kid*, a young boy, Daniel, who has been bullied at school, goes to a wise karate teacher, Mr. Miyagi, and begs him to teach him the art of karate. Mr. Miyagi, who is somewhat reluctant to take Daniel on, agrees and starts his training by having him wash and wax his car. In his serious Japanese accent, Mr. Miyagi repeats his mantra, "Wax on, wax off," while Daniel waxes in a circular motion one way and then, in taking the wax off, reverses the motion. Daniel is first stunned and then annoyed at this monotonous activity, but later realizes that this practice has forced him into a habit of defensive action to deflect punches.

Often the beginning of virtue is not understanding but action, although understanding must eventually emerge for the virtue to take root. Sometimes our desire to understand more fully is in truth an unconscious strategy for avoiding the moment of actually committing to a course of action and embarking on it.[1] We are prone to posing an endless series of questions, how and why, as if the answer to each might somehow equip us to step confidently into the future. The real obstacle to our acting, however, is not the absence of adequate information, but rather the fear of acting in the face of the inevitable uncertainty of what consequences might follow from our decisions and actions.

This, of course, is the power of the practice-based approach—the power of a courageous "yes" in the face of uncertainty as we move from anxious wondering to doing. Vince faced the prospect of actually placing the phone call to his two former employees with something approaching dread. In the days leading up to his actually making these phone calls, any abstract insights about why these calls might be important, even edifying, were utterly overwhelmed by his fears of calling the two women. Placing the calls was not in any true sense an act of rational clarity; rather, it was an exercise of volition and courage, the power of "yes" in the presence of uncertainty. It was only through the experience of making the calls, particularly the more difficult call to the second woman, that Vince began to understand the value of following-up with laid-off employees.

Yet, if practice is to yield the fruit of spiritual growth, its significance must be appropriated through personal and communal reflection that enables us to name and claim the deepest meanings of our experience. In the absence of such disciplined reflection, the unexamined experience of practice may fail to bear the fruit of virtue. It is through intentionally exploring the relationship of our lived experience to our highest ideals that we strengthen our sense of connection to these truths.

Vince could have easily disconnected the act of calling these women from the virtues of compassion and reconciliation by relegating them in his own mind to a distasteful experience of simply "following orders." He could have said "yes" to the practice and cared little about the "why" of doing it. He could have simply gone through the motions, something that seemingly happened in previous years at Tomasso.

What was it, then, that enabled Vince to appropriate the significance of this experience at a deeper level? While management practices are a powerful vehicle for embodying values within the life of the organization, commitment to these practices will break down if leaders and employees do not persuasively and consistently articulate their connection to explicit values. In the absence of continually recognizing the connection of the practices to compelling values—linking "yes" to "why"—practices risk devolving into unconscious activism. When this happens, even the best practices are capable of poisoning the culture of the organization. Vince discussed the experience with his wife and Rob MacKenzie and later articulated the impact it had on him to others in the company. It was these discussions that seemed to cement the value of the practice and transform the experience into something that changed him. He had participated in a process that linked "yes" to "why," which created the conditions for virtue, that habit of mind that makes us good as persons.[2]

Before he hired Rob MacKenzie to lead Tomasso, Ouimet had instructed previous management to implement some of the practices. Employees realized that there was limited commitment on the part of management to carry out these practices, and the practices were experienced as burdensome obligations rather than as expressions of a clear and compelling philosophy of how the company should be operated. Vince himself experienced the burdensome character of having to call the two women, but the practice became a virtue by becoming internalized. While one may come to one's duty in obedience, if one does not also begin to move toward love, such obedience can lead to rigidity, minimalism, and legalism. Simply doing one's duty as an extrinsic obligation will turn into a love grown cold.[3] Just as abstract values lack transformative power apart from practices, the opposite is also true. Practices without a reflective intentionality toward the end can result in resentment and cynicism.

When Is an Economic Reason to Lay Off an Employee a Moral Reason?

Tomasso had a rich and emerging practice-based approach to integrating spiritual and human values with the complex demands of economic performance. Its approach offered an extensive menu of management practices designed to complement and perhaps compensate for the potential excesses of what otherwise might have been a single-minded preoccupation with the sole bottom line of financial performance. Nearly all of the practices advanced by Our Project were designed to strengthen either spiritual or human growth within the life of the Tomasso organization. However, this segregation of management practices that strengthen human, community, and spiritual values from those practices that strengthen productivity and economic performance might have unintentionally reinforced the familiar and unhelpful dualism between the spiritual and the material.

Operational proficiency, superb quality, and financial success were all related, not only to the viability of Tomasso as a sustainable organization, but also to employee satisfaction with the purpose and quality of the work they did together at Tomasso. And yet there were no practices on this list whose primary focus was to strengthen the financial or productive capacities and performance of Tomasso as an economic organization.

The emphasis on practices in the areas of spiritual and human growth made perfect sense as a corrective to the traditional imbalances of economic organizations, but taken alone, these values also represented a limited understanding of organizational faithfulness. One definition of heresy is to mistake a partial truth for the whole truth. The whole truth about Tomasso was that in order for it to be healthy and serve faithfully over time, it needed to tend adequately to its financial life *and* its operational performance *and* the spiritual and human well-being of the men and women who together formed Tomasso's workplace community.

Of course, Ouimet, MacKenzie, Vince, and others knew that they needed practices that enabled them to support a financially disciplined organization. Ouimet spoke of the economic, human, and spiritual pillars of the organization; yet, it was the human and spiritual practices that seemed to get most of the attention in Our Project. It would have been prudent to have the human, spiritual, *and economic* dimensions be positively reflected in Tomasso's list of practices and values. Otherwise, every time Tomasso's managers made difficult decisions that confronted the tension between the needs of employees and the needs of financial and business realities, Tomasso's leadership would be vulnerable to the perception that they were somehow compromising or betraying Tomasso's true values. In fact, faithfulness for Tomasso would inevitably involve balancing the tension that exists between these legitimate values (some financial, some human, and some spiritual).

But there was an even deeper problem at work than balance and tension. It was the issue of integration. When the decision was made to lay off two women for economic reasons, these were the questions that needed to arise: When is an economic reason moral? What level of financial difficulty represents the threshold that legitimates the elimination of jobs (people) as an acceptable remedial strategy? How far do you bring down profits before resorting to layoffs? How long and how much should a company sacrifice financially in order to protect the jobs of dedicated employees? When is it too soon? When is it too late? What are the possibilities of retraining employees when skill sets change?

In the "just war" tradition, there is a principle of the last alternative, that one should go to war only after exhausting all other peaceful possibilities. This principle recognizes that war is not simply a political decision: it is a moral decision. Similarly, layoffs, because of their resulting emotional and financial impact on people, should be a last alternative. And even when layoffs are seen as the alternative of last resort, one of the dangers of regarding layoffs as a purely economic decision is that it appears to suggest that the outcome is somehow inevitable. Yet, in truth, in the Tomasso case, there might have been poor management decisions that contributed to the situation, resulting in a lot of pain for the two women who were laid off. So there might have been not only a need for reconciliation, but also a need for confession.

In instances when potential layoffs are caused by economic pressures, we find ourselves at the nexus of human and economic dimensions. It is not easy to determine when an economic reason is moral, but the question itself is a sign of a much deeper integration of faith and work than the compartmentalized illusion that one can segment economic questions and answers from moral ones.

Call and Compliance: Difference between Evangelizing and Proselytizing

To his great credit, Robert Ouimet articulated a clear dis-tinction between the kind of compliance Tomasso reasonably expected from its managers and employees around required stan-dards of workplace performance and practice, and the kind of "yes" that communicated genuine consent in the realms of interper-sonal relationships and spiritual practices. On the one hand, an employer can legitimately require the first kind of "yes" (compli-ance) as a condition of employment. Obviously, when it comes to the unambiguous commitment to legal accounting practices and the disciplined pursuit of operational excellence and customer service, these expectations are built into job descriptions as per-formance standards and requirements. Even beyond the legal and economic expectations, certain other practices, such as following up with laid-off employees, may be mandatory. Vince was not given a choice in the matter. It was part of his job description.

On the other hand, Ouimet steadfastly insisted that when it came to invitations around spiritual matters, only a "yes" that reflected a genuine desire and consent on the part of the employee was desirable or acceptable. There are a couple of examples of this that illustrate both the nature of this desire for an authentic "yes" and the difficult challenge this sometimes posed to Tomasso's employees.

One example was the establishment of a "silent room" at Tomasso, set aside for employees of all spiritual and philosophical persuasions as a space for prayer, meditation, and reflection. In creating this space, Ouimet sincerely desired to make possible the opportunity for such prayer or meditation to any employee who might desire it, without creating an atmosphere in which employ-ees would feel obligated to use the room in order to meet the expectation of Ouimet or other superiors. The intent was to cre-ate a space for spiritual engagement within Tomasso's facility *with-out* coercing anyone to use it. The people who tended to use the room more than most were Muslims, since their faith requires them to pray five times a day.

A second example of the challenge was the establishment of a spiritual support group. This group gathered at Ouimet's corporate offices for a time of Christian worship and reflection. Once again, Ouimet's desire was to extend an invitation to employees to share in this time in a way that welcomed *but did not coerce* their participation. To underscore the sincerity of his intent that employees freely choose their response to this invitation, Ouimet recalled an instance of inviting one of Tomasso's management team to participate. "I welcome your participation," Ouimet said, "but if I ever find out that you said yes because you thought you had to, I'll fire you!"

What Ouimet was attempting to do was *evangelize* without *proselytizing*.[4] For many, these two words are conflated, but for Ouimet they meant two very different things. To evangelize is to bring the gospel, the good news, into all dimensions of our humanity, including the world of work. Ouimet's faith demanded him to humanize the world of work and not simply to enhance his pocketbook. Ouimet attempted to find creative ways for people to develop as whole persons in the work they do. This included fostering virtue, reconciliation, training and development, just wages, good working conditions, a cooperative atmosphere, freedom to bring their spiritual selves to work, and so on. For Ouimet, to evangelize was to move away from maximizing his own shareholder wealth to building a community of work in which people could develop.

To proselytize, however, is to use the workplace as a means to impose upon others through subtle and not-so-subtle ways one's own belief system. It fails to respect the religious liberty of others and fails to create conditions for people to be authentic. Although Ouimet wanted to evangelize and not proselytize, the distinction is too often misunderstood and messy in practice. The possibility of coercion was real, *even if it was not intended*, simply because of the reality of the power and authority of Ouimet's organizational role as the one extending the invitation. Saying "no" to some of the spiritual practices involved the perceived risk of disappointing one's employer and being passed up for promotions and rewards. This concern resonated with the confusion on the part of some employees about whether there was a hidden religious agenda underlying these activities, a thinly veiled desire to proselytize them.

This, of course, is why some people argue for the strict separation between faith and work. It was well and fine that Ouimet should create conditions for employees to develop, but the explicit reference to religious language in the workplace will always run the danger of violating the conscience of its workers.

But for Ouimet, the "keystone," the arch that held together the economic and moral pillars of the company, was spiritual and religious.[5] Without a spiritual keystone—a bridge of transcendence, love, faith, prayer, silence, meditation, and so on, that drew upon grace and spiritual sustenance—the moral practices of the project would be swept aside, and worse, determined only by the economic and competitive pressures of running a business. For example, this current case study involving Vince would never have occurred if Ouimet did not believe in the importance of spiritual reconciliation that was nurtured in him through the sacrament of reconciliation. To cut off the spiritual and religious sources of these practices would be to undermine the very uniqueness of the kind of company Tomasso was striving to be.

Conclusion

The purpose of the practices that Ouimet developed at Tomasso was to more fully embody revered values within the day-to-day life of the organization. The instance in which Vince followed up with discharged employees gave concrete expression to the value of reconciliation and a deep solidarity with those who were no longer with the company. If employees were seen as merely human capital, there would be no need to follow up with them, but if they were seen as *persons*, endowed with human dignity and made in the image of God, then the relationship between managers and laid-off employees demanded the use of compelling practices that genuinely reflected the values of solidarity and reconciliation.

These deep connections between practice and belief are looked upon with suspicion and unease by the wider culture. Ouimet was advised more than once to secularize his language because of the increasing pluralism and diversity of society. He found such advice to be its own form of social conformism, which had become rapidly pervasive in Quebec society. Ouimet explained that "it is in the name of secularism that most economic and political leaders believe they cannot make public their most deeply held, personal convictions, especially if they are spiritual and religious in nature."[6] Thus, business institutions start to look alike, and instead of promoting diversity, secularism has actually reduced pluralism, and especially institutional pluralism, by prohibiting religious and spiritual influences, which, as it was done in Tomasso, create unique and humanizing organizational practices.

Ouimet saw these practices as an experiment, and with any experiment, one has to try things out of the ordinary. Instead of driving the company to the lowest common-values denominator, which tends to be safe and secular, but rather bland and uninspiring, Ouimet was inviting people to speak from their deepest center, but in such a way that encouraged everyone to do the same. Ouimet and Tomasso's leadership sought to nurture an environment in which it became increasingly possible to bring one's whole self to work without fear of coercing or being coerced. It may also have created the conditions for an authentic institutional pluralism that allows a business to express itself in new and creative ways.

CONCLUSION

CONCLUSION

The Business of Practical Wisdom

Where is the wisdom we have lost in knowledge?
Where is the knowledge we have lost in information?

T. S. ELIOT[1]

Eliot's poetry captures a significant temptation within business. When leaders and their organizations fail to guide their information and knowledge toward wise decision making, they see only parts and not the whole. They zoom in on decisions, but their lens gets stuck and they cannot zoom back out to see the broader landscape.

Plagued by a financial crisis, recessions, accounting scandals, and business corruption, our short time in the twenty-first century has taught us an age-old lesson that we seemingly tend to forget: leaders without wisdom make for a very dangerous world. Managing organizations takes a great deal of information, knowledge, skill, and technique; yet by themselves, these management techniques do not tell us whether the organization and leaders are good or corrupt. Nazis have shown us what "highly skilled barbar-

117

ians" look like. Our most recent financial crisis has shown us what "highly skilled technicians" look like.

For the most part, the perpetrators of our recent financial crisis were neither vicious nor cutthroat; rather, they were people who lacked moral character, who demonstrated moral thought-lessness, who felt entitled to their "fair share" (and possibly more), who rationalized their behavior, and who blindly followed the money. Consumers, loan officers, investment bankers, and speculators all attempted to capitalize within a particular part of the financial system; in so doing, each myopically passed on problems to other parts of that system. These people were technically competent, hardworking, and for the most part law-abiding, but wisdom to see their role in a broader, destructive whole escaped them.

This is not true of all businesses, however. Not all leaders are self-interested utility maximizers, as indicated in most Economics 101 textbooks. Not all firms see their purpose as maximizing share-holder wealth, as indicated in most Finance 101 textbooks. Business is not a monolithic entity. If it were, we would have seen long ago a total collapse of our economy. Fortunately, we still have thousands of leaders and firms whose moral and spiritual centers are defined by more than just economic incentives, legal constraints, and individualistic preferences.

The leaders in this book were—and are—trying to build good companies. They were trying to be wise in practical affairs—what the Christian tradition calls the virtue of *practical wisdom*. This virtue is considered sine qua non for business leaders. It is that inner habit and quality of the leader that integrates effective means and good ends in changing and unique circumstances.

At the heart of practical wisdom is the ability to *see things whole*. It is not about achieving simply one good, such as profit, but about achieving a good life overall. For leaders, part of this good life is being faithful to their deepest beliefs and not compartmentalizing them to Sunday morning. Such leaders want a good company that treats its coworkers well (identity/culture), that serves its customers' needs (purpose/mission), and that produces a healthy profit for its owners (stewardship/fiduciary). These goals as a whole are not easily achieved. Yet, this is the place where businesspeople live, and it is their vocation to build institutions that serve not just their particular good, but the common good.

Such leaders want this wisdom to be incarnated in concrete practices and policies, not just in abstract mission statements. This is what makes it *practical* wisdom. These leaders are trying to be wise in institutionalizing effective practices that foster right relationships. Robert Ouimet from Tomasso, for example, was particularly explicit that faith has to be embodied in distinct practices that can carry human and spiritual values in a way that humanizes the organization. Faith without works—without practices—is dead (Jas 2:17).

So how do we know when leaders have practical wisdom, and what lessons can we learn from observing their practice of this virtue? There is no formula for practical wisdom, no five-point checklist. But there are indicators of its presence. Cicero explains the parts of practical wisdom in terms of time: "*memory* of the past, *understanding* of the present, and *foresight* in regard to the future."[2] The practically wise leader feels rooted in the past and connected to the future, which makes the decision in the present of grave importance. When the leaders in this book were facing a decision, their wisdom or lack of it was premised on their memory and reflection, how they took counsel to understand the situation they were in, and how well they were able to look into the future to see the implications of their decision. What made them practically wise was that they saw holistically, rather than in parts.

Our origins, presence, and destiny are critical interdependent moments of time. The practical, wise leader needs hindsight and foresight to have insight. For we do not know who we are unless we know where we have come from and where we are going. By reflecting upon these parts of time in light of the three cases we have examined, we see three key lessons for faithful leaders who want to be practically wise.

Lesson 1. Take Time to *Remember*

An important conviction of Christian faith is that there is a law written on our hearts not of our own making (Rom 2:14 ff). It is a law that we cannot completely forget, although we can repress and ignore it. Because we are created in God's image, we have a deep "moral and spiritual DNA." There is in each person a deep memory of what is true and good about what it means to be a human being, a memory that haunts us to build community, to practice virtue, and to make the world a better place. Robert Greenleaf and others remind us that the very word *religion* (*religio*, meaning "to bind together") is all about re-membering, reintegrating that which has disintegrated.

This memory is not a list of rules of do's and don'ts, or some kind of store of retrievable data. It is "an inner sense, a capacity to recall, so that the one whom it addresses, if he is not turned in on himself, hears its echo from within. He sees: 'That's it! That is what my nature points to and seeks.'"[3] When we are at our best we remember this deep, created purpose within us. Yet, we are not always at our best and we too often forget the purpose of the trip. Financial and operational pressures of declining revenue, shrinking profit margins, operational bottlenecks, long workdays, and so on, can swamp even the best of leaders to forget their God-given purpose. This is a forgetfulness, not of facts, but of *being*—of being human.

We all need help to remember what is best within us, help that comes not only from work itself, but also from our nonwork lives: our families, churches, schools, and wider culture. The deeper humanity of the leaders in this book was cultivated in the cultural institutions of family, religion, and education. Through familial relationships, silence, reflection on scripture, prayer, worship, study, and the like, these leaders engaged this deeper DNA that informed how they worked in their companies. Embedded in a rich moral and spiritual formation, the leaders in this book looked at their work and their companies with a deep sense of vocation and calling. This nonwork experience helped them to "remember" a deeper reality that would not have been immediately present to them in their day-to-day business decisions.

As the founders of Reell started their company, the scriptures reminded them of the deep human and spiritual relations that should inform how they ran their company. The Golden Rule ("Treat others as you would like to be treated") was not simply a vague disembodied platitude, but a powerful and authoritative principle of faith that guided them in how to treat employees in times of retrenchment. It helped them to formulate a last-alternative layoff policy, because that's how people want to be treated. They also created a target wage (living wage), an employee ownership program, open-book management, commitment to the community, and other programs and professional postures based upon their clear understanding of what it means to be spiritual human beings. They experienced that sense of "That's it. That's how we should run our company." They didn't forget this when economic pressures were bearing down on them. They remained steady and faithful to this deep memory God imprinted upon their souls. They sacrificed profit, reduced wages, and recalibrated their company for a period of time to weather the economic storm so as to remain a community of persons.

In a rather different way, Earl Stevens from Engineering Products (EP) and Robert Ouimet came to realize that they were at risk of becoming disconnected from the purpose of their life and work. They experienced a divided life compartmentalized by different moral and behavioral standards for faith and for work, and they said, "No, this is not how we live our lives. This is not it!"

For Stevens, his church in particular helped him to remember the purpose of the trip. It reminded him through fellowship, sermons, worship bulletins, prayers of the faithful, and faith-formation programs that he was a "minister to the world." This gave him the courage to go beyond just productivity techniques, and he began to introduce management materials from Peter Senge, Stephen Covey, and eventually Seeing Things Whole, which brought a deeper meaning to his work as well as to those within the company.

For Ouimet, his Catholic education played an important part in helping him to remember the deeper reality of his work. He took a sabbatical, went to Catholic University in Fribourg, Switzerland, and studied theology and Catholic social thought, which helped him integrate his faith and business. It was here that he began to reflect upon and understand a more systematic understanding of practices in his organization. His intentional study gave him time to remember.

A strong family and faith life, along with a good education, created a contemplative outlook for these leaders that reminded them of the deepest realities, which can become hidden by the pressures and problems of business. This outlook enables all of us to still see the world with wonderment, with awe. It gives us eyes to see life's deeper meaning, to experience others not as things to be used, but as persons with whom to build relationships. "It is the outlook of those who do not presume to take possession of reality but instead accept it as a gift, discovering in all things the reflection of the Creator and seeing in every person his living image (cf. Gen 1:27; Ps 8:5)."[4] It is an outlook that creates—not wishful thinking about how important and glorified and successful we might be in *this* world—but the conditions for a silent, unbiased perception to remember who we are in the real world as created, loved and redeemed by God.

Lesson 2. Seek Wise Counsel

Leaders need counsel. Few people would disagree with this, but it may not always be clear why this is the case. Machiavelli believed that the leader needs counsel, not to be wise, but to hold, acquire, and expand his power. This is not wisdom but a cunning vice of careerism. When we speak of counsel for the practically wise leader, we need to see it as a process of *co-knowing* with others and *the* Other to achieve the good in practical affairs. This requires far more discernment than any individual leader possesses.

CONCLUSION: The Business of Practical Wisdom

Practical wisdom is not just about knowing the good, but about getting the good done in a particular situation. Leaders in the case studies of this book needed counsel not just on ends, principles, or values, but more often on the *means* to good ends. Not just on universals, but on particulars. The leaders within this book desired to act holistically and faithfully; yet, they were constantly puzzled by how to do it, not so much in terms of principle, but in terms of the concrete means to achieve the good in the here and now. Do we lay off people or take pay cuts at this time? Do we communicate the bad news to employees? Do we lower our price on this product in hope of acquiring more business? Do we expand in this market or that market? Do we diversify our customer base at the risk of compromising our service to our current customers? Do we implement this inventory system or another?

These are not just technical decisions, but moral ones, because they have significant consequences for the culture, mission, and sustainability of the company. Yet, these decisions are far from clear at the time when they have to be made. Leaders have in front of them not just one or two possibilities, but multiple possibilities, all of which are contingent on variables that have significant implications into the future. But they have to make decisions in the present. This is why they need counsel.

EP formalized their counsel by participating in Seeing Things Whole roundtables. The *STW* roundtables serve as a form of external counsel by bringing together a community of business leaders who hold one another's organizations in trust. Roundtables are geographically based, with gatherings taking place on a rotating basis in one another's business settings. In each instance, the host organization presents a real-time, unresolved challenge it is facing, and participants serve as temporary trustees who work for half a day with the hosts on this dilemma. In their role as temporary trustees, they bring a "balcony perspective" rooted in their own life experience and drawing upon their own personal moral, spiritual, and religious centers. They ask purposeful and broad questions: What carries the weight of a real relationship in regard to this or that particular practice and policy? How does the organization address and resolve this challenge in a way that it becomes a stronger community of persons? What will it entail to make the situation and the people within it whole? What might it look like for an organization to face this challenge in a way that reflects its best and most heroic possibilities?

When the leaders of Reell were discerning whether to lay off or cut wages, they also sought counsel from those lower within the organization. They were not abdicating their authority through a majority-opinion vote, but they sought consultation from others. This generated a robust debate among those within Reell. The questions of how far down the organization one goes and for how long does one allow the debate to go on, and so on, are all practical considerations that will depend on the nature of the decision and other extenuating circumstances.

Ouimet built into his organization several dimensions of counsel, but most intriguing was how he integrated spiritual counsel, and in particular silence, into his organization. One of the counsels Ouimet received from Mother Teresa was to implement a room for silence in his plant. As we mentioned in the case, this was not well received by all the managers of his company. One manager in particular was quite hostile to it since he saw it as a haven for lazy employees and a wasteful use of space; he also thought it possessed a whiff of religious posturing, which had little place within a business. While this manager vowed never to go into such a room, even he eventually admitted that such a room influenced him to go into his own office to take his own silence, to think about decisions, and to ponder their implications.

To create time and space for such counsel is itself a moral act, not at all easy in the pressurized and fast-paced environment facing today's institutions. Time is money, customers are impatient, market conditions change quickly. On this point, Aristotle advised to be quick in carrying out the counsel taken, but slow in taking it.[5] By taking counsel, by gathering the advice of others, a leader is creating time to make a thoughtful, wise decision. Wisdom demands a holistic approach, not a mechanistic one, and this takes time. But a wise leader will also be aware of the time they create for decision making. Leaders who take counsel must not be too slow in implementing counsel. Often, the longer that leaders take in making decisions, the fewer options they have. While counsel is important and it takes time to receive it, practically wise leaders must be shrewd and bold enough to know when quick, decisive action is necessary.

Lesson 3. Have the End in Mind: Foresight

One of most difficult and anxiety-producing dimensions of a leader's life is foresight—that ability to have the end in mind so as to bring about a future good that does not currently exist.[6] To be wise in day-to-day affairs is to discern "the end in every beginning."[7] Wise leaders see further into reality because they recognize that something enduring is at stake in the actions they are performing. Yet, having the end in mind cannot happen unless we see in the concrete decisions of today—whether they be firing an employee, dealing with demands from customers, addressing production problems, and so forth—that something lasting is occurring in these actions. We see that, in our actions today, there is a future emerging that makes those actions of today a prime indicator of our destiny. It is this insight into this future state that we call *foresight*.

We all make decisions because we want to achieve some perceived good. The fact that we never do anything unless we want to achieve some end or outcome is something so obvious that we rarely even think about it. But we need to think about it; otherwise, we may end up in a place where we regretfully realize that we have few choices. Robert Greenleaf observed that the "action which society labels 'unethical' in the present moment is often really one of no choice. By this standard, a lot of guilty people are walking around with an air of innocence that they would not have if society were able always to pin a label 'unethical' on the failure to foresee and the conscious failure to act constructively when there was freedom to act."[8] To be wise is to have a long-term perspective, to see the big picture, to look beyond the immediate situation. It entails the ability to take all relevant circumstances into account and anticipate unintended consequences.

When Ouimet at Tomasso created the policy of following up with fired or laid-off employees, he was anticipating the importance of reconciliation. He saw that the heart of his company was not maximizing shareholder wealth or balancing stakeholder interests; rather, it was a community of persons whose work was to serve the common good. This was achieved not by wishing it, but by practicing policies that built it. This kind of company is developed through practices that foster right relationships. When people are fired or laid off, these relationships are strained and damaged. If these relationships are not reconciled, their lingering residue adversely affects other relationships. The more of these unreconciled relationships there are within a company's sphere, the harder it is to create a community of persons within and without the company. Ouimet anticipated a future that would be built upon reconciled relationships, and thus created a culture where persons flourish.

As much as we would like to predict the future, of course we can't. As seen in the Reell case, the leaders could not predict with 100 percent accuracy whether demand for their product would return after the 2000–2001 recession. They certainly could not have anticipated the terrorist attack of 9/11, nor its long-reaching economic implications. Foresight does not take away the vulnerability of an unknown future. Yet, it does depend upon hindsight. Even though the past does not dictate the future, we too often fail to learn from our mistakes and forget life's lessons. Bob Carlson from Reell remembered that the layoff of a former employer significantly damaged the culture of that organization. He foresaw a future possibility precisely because he remembered his past experience.

While leaders cannot predict the future, they do, nonetheless, have to anticipate it. When EP was riding the growth wave of its customers, it knew that something was not quite right. It saw the warning signs of the draconian measures that GM was placing on other suppliers, but because they were not initially affected by it, and because growth was keeping them busy, they ignored the warning signs before them. Riding the wave is the time to prepare for potential downsides—to anticipate future problems. It is this intuition that a leader needs to cultivate because more options for preparation and development are available during periods of great growth and success. As time passes, however, options may disappear. EP did not succeed in widening its customer base and remained too dependent on the three American automakers. While it may be too much to expect executives at EP to have predicted the trend of draconian measures of the whole U.S. auto industry, it does highlight how important it is for leaders to read early warning signs, especially when a company is healthy.

Foresight is usually most needed when things are going well, not when they are going badly. Machiavelli, though he is not generally a good source for practical wisdom, was right when he observed that it is easier to cure a disease at its beginning, although harder to detect, "but as time passes, not having been treated or recognized at the outset, it becomes easy to diagnose but difficult to cure."[9]

While in some ways we are better at predicting future consequences than we were in the past, we are not gods or fortunetellers. Our advances in science and technology cannot capture the unpredictability of an unwieldy future. We are called with foresight to manage future risk and reduce it, but we cannot eliminate it. Yet, this inability to read the future perfectly does not cast us into a dark and dismal future; rather, it points to a mysterious and wonderful dependence on God, which enriches our lives and the meaning of being human.

One Last Thought: A Caution

Our point of this final chapter is to emphasize the importance of practical wisdom in discerning good decisions that build good companies that serve the common good. Practical wisdom is a necessary virtue for all leaders who care about more than their own careers and self-interests. Yet, its achievement may find the leader tempted by what the Christian tradition calls the most dangerous of vices: *pride*.[10] Pride, that radical individualism, creates an illusion of autonomy that is a constant temptation for the business leader, and nothing short of God's grace will correct this.

Pride is often stimulated when the leader meets success. The achievements of business leaders will always be prone to be interpreted as their own, and such achievements lose their connection to the deeper reality of the Christian story. Pride tells us that our achievement is not a participation in creation, not prone to sin, and not in need of redemption. Pride makes the claim, "This is my achievement! Behold and admire me!" Of course, it is usually more subtle than this and often camouflaged in false humility. Ironically, prudent leaders are most susceptible to pride precisely because at every success they will be tempted to think they are the source of their own moral rectitude, insight, and achievement.

People of faith are also particularly prone to this temptation. They see themselves as spiritually centered, morally upright, emotionally balanced, and economically successful. They believe they have figured out the formula to life and thus think rather well of themselves. It is precisely at this point that they are most in danger, since they fool themselves, in subtle ways, to believe that *they* have achieved their success, their status, their development.

In the parable of the tax collector and the Pharisee, the Gospel warns of those "who were confident of their own righteousness" (Luke 18:9–14). Jesus had great compassion for those sinners who were often plagued by ugly and obvious vices, like greed, lust, and gluttony. He taught that though these sins do significant damage in the world, they are not the most dangerous sins. Because they drive us to our base desires, we tend to see them as vices not virtues. We who wallow in them recognize their destruction within us. Jesus, however, had harsher medicine for those who were afflicted with sins of pride, self-righteousness, envy, and lack of compassion. These traits were more damaging because they were more easily hidden, rationalized, and even disguised as virtues. This is why, as Josef Pieper explained, it "is not the 'sinners' but the 'prudent ones' who are most liable to close themselves off" from a life of grace.[11] When prudence or practical wisdom is cut off from a deep sense that our achievements are not our own, we will begin to move toward pride and all of the spiritual distortion and destruction that accompanies it.

We opened this chapter with a quote from T. S. Eliot reflecting on how information and knowledge must be ordered toward wisdom. We now close this chapter with the insight that wisdom, in order to resist this temptation of pride over a lifetime, must be ordered to charity, that grace of a love that is "received and given."[12] The practical, wise leader will have an intrinsic human need for the purifying, elevating action of divine love. This love, which is first received, always breeds gratitude and not pride and entitlement. This is why we come to the deepest sense of ourselves not through what we achieve but what we receive. This receptivity is a grace of God's love given to us in talents, interests, desires, and skills, which are to be given in return for the good of the world. Our identity as persons is to respond to the gifts that have been first given, to make of ourselves a self-gift inspired by and in cooperation with divine grace.

The leaders in this book are faithful leaders, not perfect leaders, because they have a deep sense that their talents and the successes of their companies are not theirs alone. Without this gratitude for what has been received in grace and love, it is doubtful that Reell would have taken the time and made the sacrifice incumbent in that choice to save jobs. It would be highly improbable that Tomasso would seek reconciliation with its former employees, or that EP would have taken the care to communicate and confess their mistakes to their employees. These practices, along with their ability to see things whole, were born from a call among these leaders to create bonds of connection that bind people together as a community of persons. As these leaders set in motion such practices, employees, customers, and suppliers often, although not always, responded in kind. This reciprocal relationship, this receiving and giving, endows business with a human form that creates conditions for people to flourish and develop. Faithful leaders then become witnesses of action that reflect over a lifetime the image that God has imprinted upon them, an image of a community of persons where each is fulfilled in the other.

Notes

Foreword

1. Robert K. Greenleaf, *Servant Leadership: A Journey into the Nature of Legitimate Power and Greatness*, ed., Larry Spears (New York/Mahwah, NJ: Paulist Press, 2002), 62.

2. Ibid., 27.

3. Jitsuo Morikawa, quoted in Richard Broholm, "Trustees of the Universe: Recovering the Whole Ministry of the People of God," www.seeingthingswhole.org/uploads/STW-Trustee-of-the-Universe_567684.pdf, page 13. Accessed March 29, 2011.

4. Robert K. Greenleaf, *Seeker and Servant: Reflections on Religious Leadership*, ed. Anne T. Fraker and Larry Spears (Hoboken, NJ: Jossey-Bass, Inc., 1996), 192.

Introduction: Telling the Whole Story

1. Robert K. Greenleaf, *Seeker and Servant: Reflections on Religious Leadership*, ed. Anne T. Fraker and Larry Spears (Hoboken, NJ: Jossey-Bass, Inc., 1996), 191–92.

2. There are exceptions to this. See Kenneth E. Goodpaster, Laura L. Nash, and Henri-Claude de Bettignies, eds., *Business Ethics: Policies and Persons* 4th ed. (Columbus, OH: McGraw Hill, 2005), 151–66.

3. For background on some of these companies and their lead-ers, see Patrick Murphy and Georges Enderle, "Managerial Ethical Leadership," *Business Ethics Quarterly* 5.1 (1995): 117–28.

4. This phrase comes from David Walsh, founder of the National Institute on Media and the Family.

5. Hans Urs von Balthasar, *The Christian State of Life* (San Francisco: Ignatius Press, 1983), 48.

6. Quoted in John Kavanaugh, *Following Christ in a Consumer Society: The Spirituality of Cultural Resistance* (Maryknoll, NY: Orbis Books, 2000), 11.

Reell Precision Manufacturing: The Case

1. For a fuller discussion on tensions over the spiritual char-acter of Reell, see Kenneth E. Goodpaster, Laura L. Nash, and Henri-Claude de Bettignies, eds., *Business Ethics: Policies and Persons* 4th ed. (Columbus, OH: McGraw Hill, 2005).

2. We are grateful to Stan Nyquist, former board chair of Reell, who provided this information.

3. Wahlstedt later reflected that always going in with the best price firmly fixed did not always serve the company well because it did not allow for negotiation. In light of the current norm on price negotiations, he probably would have padded the price offer and allowed for reductions.

4. In the 1990s, Reell's growth area went from rotary motion devices found in copiers to hinges in laptop computers. This brought significant growth but also turmoil in terms of significant price reductions in computers, shortened life span of computers placing greater demands on new product development, erratic increases and decreases in demand, and the movement of produc-tion of computers to China.

Reell Precision Manufacturing: A Reflection

1. For a description of the threefold model see http://www.seeingthingswhole.org/uploads/Three-Fold-Model-Organization_

442059.pdf (accessed May 14, 2010). While Reell management preferred the word *mission*, the originators of the model, David Specht and Dick Broholm, use the term *purpose*.

2. Ken Goodpaster, "Ethics or Excellence? Conscience as a Check on the Unbalanced Pursuit of Organizational Goals," *Ivey Business Journal* (March–April 2004): 6–9.

3. STW's threefold model of organizational life posits the potential of a shadow expression of each of the organization's three dimensions. The shadow refers to the unhealthy or destructive possibilities associated with each of these dimensions, including those that can result from any of the dimensions becoming inflated at the expense of the other dimensions. This is consistent with an early church definition of heresy as the error of mistaking a partial truth as the whole truth.

4. The "Lake Wobegon Effect" comes from Garrison Keillor's radio show about a fictional Minnesota town where "all the women are strong, all the men are good looking, and all the children are above average."

5. This image of the stool came from Bob G. Wahlstedt, a coworker at Reell and the son of one of its founders.

Ten Years Later

1. Bo Burlingham, "Paradise Lost," *Inc.* magazine, February 1, 2008, archived at http://www.inc.com/magazine/20080201/paradise-lost.html.

Engineered Products: The Case

1. We are grateful for Ed Mosel's invaluable assistance on this case.

2. "Engineered Products" is a pseudonym for a real company. The information contained in the case study is about real issues with only the names being changed at the request of the organization.

3. Dick Broholm was a fellow church member and had helped to found an organization named Seeing Things Whole, which focused on exploring the intersection of faith, values, and organizational life. Broholm was also the founding director of the Greenleaf Center.

4. For more information on STW's threefold model, see David L. Specht and Richard R. Broholm, "Toward a Theology of Institutions," in *Practicing Servant Leadership: Succeeding Through Trust, Bravery and Forgiveness*, Larry C. Spears and Michele Lawrence (Hoboken, NJ: Jossey-Bass, 2004), 167; also David Specht and Dick Broholm, "Threefold Model of Organizational Life: Testimonies and Queries for Seeing Things Whole," at http://www.seeingthingswhole.org/uploads/Three-Fold-Model-Organization_442059.pdf (accessed April 13, 2010).

5. Stevens adopted the language of the threefold model by replacing the language of stewardship with "fiduciary." He felt that, as a publicly traded company, this language would better fit the company's situation.

Engineered Products: A Reflection

1. See John Paul II, *Laborem exercens*, 5–6, where he discusses how the way we work has an impact on the kind of people that we are—our character and personality. In other words, work doesn't just have objective effects, like producing products and services, but it also has a subjective effect, impacting the persons within the organization. Hence, the idea of the "subjective dimension" of work.

2. See John Paul II, *Sollicitudo rei socialis*, 36–37.

Tomasso Corporation: The Case

1. In addition to Tomasso Corporation, Robert Ouimet's holding company, OCB Inc., owned several companies in the

foods sector, including Paris Paté, Esta Foods, Clark Foods, and the original family business named after Robert Ouimet's father, René Ouimet, Inc.

2. J.-Robert Ouimet, *Everything Has Been Loaned to You* (Paris: Presses de la Renaissance, 2008), 61–62.

3. The English-language Web site for Our Project is http://www.our-project.com. The complete *Golden Book* is available as a download at http:www.our-project.com/index.php?id=10 (accessed April 5, 2011).

4. Rob MacKenzie knew firsthand how difficult these follow-up conversations could be. Soon after Rob's own arrival as Tomasso's president, he dismissed several employees as part of a dramatic and ultimately successful high-stakes change effort, and had himself followed up with each of these former employees.

5. http://www.our-project.com/index.php?id=23 (accessed April 6, 2011).

Tomasso Corporation: A Reflection

1. See Peter Block, *The Answer to How Is Yes: Acting on What Matters* (San Francisco: Berrett-Koehler Publishers, Inc., 2002).

2. John Paul II, *Laborem exercens*, 9.

3. Hans Urs von Balthasar, *The Christian State of Life*, trans. Sr. Mary Frances McCarthy (San Francisco: Ignatius Press, 1983), 30–32.

4. Pope Benedict XVI, *Deus caritas est*, 31.

5. The keystone itself is described in a pluralistic way that can mean the "Creator; the Higher Power; God Love; God the Father, Son, and Holy Spirit; or any other opening to Transcendence....All actors in the company's life freely interpret the value of Transcendence in their own ways." At http://www.our-project.com/index.php?id=25 (accessed April 6, 2011).

6. J.-Robert Ouimet, *Everything Has Been Loaned to You* (Paris: Presses de la Renaissance, 2008), 97.

Conclusion:
The Business of Practical Wisdom

1. T. S. Eliot, *The Rock* (London: Faber & Faber, 1934), lines 14–15.

2. Quoted in Thomas Aquinas, *Summa Theologica* I, II, 62, art. 6.

3. See Joseph Ratzinger, "Conscience and Truth," (10th Workshop for Bishops, February 1991, Dallas), http://www.ewtn.com/library/curia/ratzcons.htm.

4. John Paul II, *Evangelium vitae*, 83.

5. Aristotle, *The Nicomachean Ethics* (Oxford: Oxford University Press, 1988), vi, 9, 149.

6. Stephen R. Covey, *The 7 Habits of Highly Effective People* (New York: Simon & Schuster, 1989), chap. 2.

7. John Henry Newman, *Discourses on the Scope and Nature of University Education* (Dublin: James Duffy, 1852), 218.

8. Robert K. Greenleaf, *Servant Leadership: A Journey into the Nature of Legitimate Power and Greatness* (Mahwah, NJ: Paulist Press, 2002), 39–40.

9. Niccolò Machiavelli, *The Prince* (New York: Oxford University Press, Inc., 1998), 12.

10. See C. S. Lewis, *Mere Christianity* (New York: The MacMillan Company, 1960), see book III, chapter 8, "The Great Sin."

11. Josef Pieper, *The Four Cardinal Virtues* (Notre Dame, IN: University of Notre Dame Press, 1966), 37.

12. Benedict XVI, *Caritas in veritate*, 5.

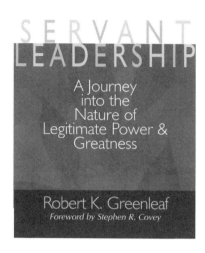

"...one of those rare books that will live beyond the life of its creator."
– James A. Autry

25th
Anniversary
Edition

SERVANT
LEADERSHIP
A Journey into the Nature of Legitimate Power & Greatness
Robert K. Greenleaf
Foreword by Stephen R. Covey

Servant Leadership

25TH ANNIVERSARY EDITION

A Journey into the Nature of Legitimate Power and Greatness

Robert K. Greenleaf

A classic work on leadership for business men and women, government leaders and all persons in positions of authority.

0-8091-0554-3 Hardcover

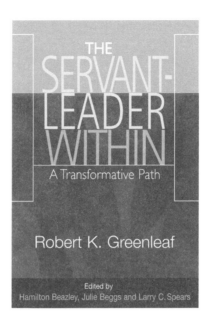

The Servant-Leader Within

A Transformative Path

**Robert K. Greenleaf; edited by Hamilton Beazley,
Julie Beggs, and Larry C. Spears**

Combines in one volume classic works on servant-leadership and
its relationship to the art of teaching and the act of learning.

0-8091-4219-8 Paperback

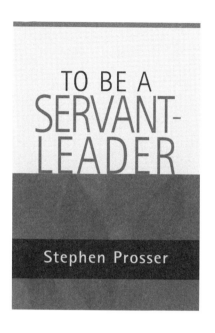

To Be a Servant-Leader

Stephen Prosser

Based upon or inspired by biblical texts,
To Be a Servant-Leader examines the main characteristics
or principles of leadership.

978-0-8091-4467-9 Paperback

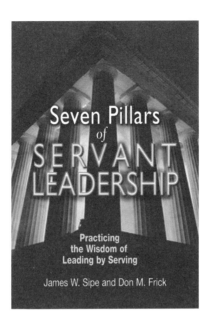

Seven Pillars of Servant Leadership

Practicing the Wisdom of Leading by Serving

James W. Sipe and Don M. Frick

Offers a skills-oriented approach to acquiring the most critical competencies of effective servant leadership, without overlooking matters of the heart and soul that make it all worthwhile.

978-0-8091-4560-7 Paperback

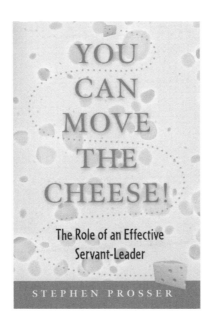

You Can Move the Cheese!

The Role of an Effective Servant-Leader

Stephen Prosser

Identifies five key people propositions, practiced by enlightened companies, and invites leaders to become purposeful, principled, resolute and exemplary as they transform their places of work and the lives of their followers.

978-0-8091-4640-6 Paperback

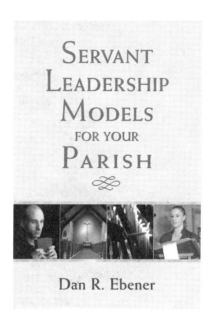

Servant Leadership Models
for Your Parish

Dan R. Ebener

Servant Leadership Models for Your Parish explores the practice
of servant leadership in a church context. It presents seven
behaviors practiced by leaders and members in high-performing
parishes and provides real-life examples of these practices.

978-0-8091-4653-6 Paperback

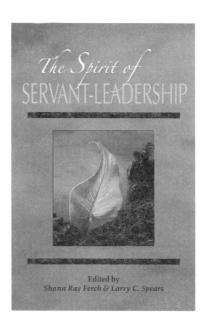

The Spirit of Servant-Leadership

Edited by Shann Ray Ferch and Larry C. Spears

In *The Spirit of Servant-Leadership* editors Shann Ferch and Larry
Spears present an elegant and powerful approach to the nature
of the leader-follower dynamic, with a specific focus on many
of the most radical, life-affirming, and transformative facets
of the servant-leader.

978-0-8091-0594-6 Hardcover

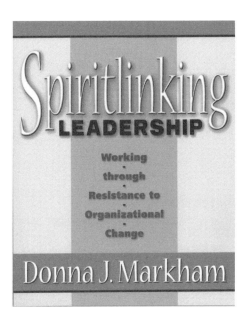

Spiritlinking Leadership

Working through Resistance to Organizational Change

Donna J. Markham

An approach to leadership that affirms each individual as
an expression of organizational energy, wisdom, spirit and
culture, and encourages trust in the collective inner wisdom
of the members of the group.

0-8091-3840-9 Paperback

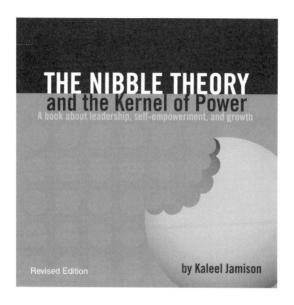

The Nibble Theory and the Kernel of Power

REVISED EDITION

A Book about Leadership, Self-Empowerment, and Personal Growth

Kaleel Jamison

This creative theory about growth and self-empowerment compares a person to a circle that has the unique ability to keep expanding.

0-8091-4187-6 Paperback

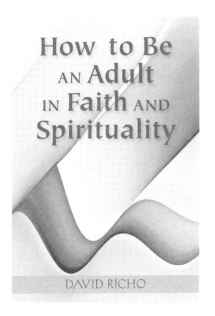

How to Be an Adult in Faith and Spirituality

David Richo

Popular best-selling author and therapist David Richo provides here a detailed and straightforward vision of what faith and spirituality can look like in adult consciousness.

978-0-8091-4691-8 Paperback

Where the Hell Is God?

Richard Leonard, SJ;
Foreword by James Martin, SJ

Combines professional insights along with the author's own
experience and insights to speculate on how believers can
make sense of their Christian faith when confronted with
tragedy and suffering.

978-1-58768-060-1 Paperback
978-0-8091-4749-6 Large Print

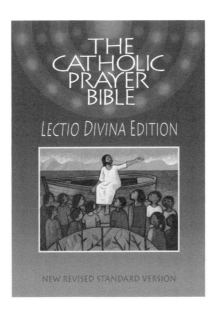

The Catholic Prayer Bible (NRSV)

Lectio Divina Edition

An ideal Bible for anyone who desires to reflect on the individual stories and chapters of just one, or even all, of the biblical books, while being led to prayer though meditation on that biblical passage.

978-0-8091-4766-3 Deluxe edition; bonded leather cover—navy; gilt page edges.

978-0-8091-4663-5 Paperback

978-0-8091-0587-8 Hardcover